Y

R(
AND THE VATICAN

Fiona Nichols

NEW
HOLLAND

★★★ Highly recommended
★★ Recommended
★ See if you can

Sixth edition published in 2013
by New Holland Publishers (UK) Ltd
London • Cape Town • Sydney • Auckland
10 9 8 7 6 5 4 3 2 1

website: www.newhollandpublishers.com

Garfield House, 86 Edgware Road
London W2 2EA, United Kingdom

Wembley Square, First Floor, Solan Road
Gardens, Cape Town 8001, South Africa

Unit 1, 66 Gibbes Street, Chatswood
NSW 2067, Australia

218 Lake Road, Northcote,
Auckland, New Zealand

Distributed in the USA by
The Globe Pequot Press, Connecticut

ISBN 978 1 78009 422 9

Acknowledgements: The aut
following people and organi
assistance: Fulvia Angelini,
Margary Martin, PierLuigi Sc
Azienda Promozione Turistic
tourist organization, Enjoy R

This guidebook has been wr
and updaters. The informatic
impartial opinion, and neither ....
accept payment in return for including in the book or

writing more favourable reviews of any of the establishments. Whilst every effort has been made to ensure that
this guidebook is as accurate and up to date as possible,
please be aware that the facts quoted are subject to
change, particularly the price of food, transport and
accommodation. The Publisher accepts no responsibility
or liability for any loss, injury or inconvenience incurred
by readers or travellers using this guide.

Publishing Manager: Thea Grobbelaar
DTP Cartographic Manager: Genené Hart
Editors: Thea Grobbelaar, Lorissa Bouwer, Carla
Redelinghuys, Alicha van Reenen, Melany Porter
Design and DTP: Nicole Bannister, Benjamin Latham
Picture Researchers: Shavonne Govender, Colette Stott
Cartographers: Tracey-Lee Fredericks, Reneé Spocter,
Lorissa Bouwer, Carryck Wise, Genené Hart, Tanja Spinola
Consultants: Melissa Shales, Liz Booth
Reproduction by Resolution (Cape Town) and Hirt & Carter
(Pty) Ltd, Cape Town. Printed and bound by Craft Print
International Ltd, Singapore.

Cover: The Colosseum by night.
Title Page: A rooftop view of Rome.

CONTENTS

1
Introducing Rome and the Vatican

If there was ever a city that earned its epithet, it is Rome. The Eternal City has witnessed and shaped 3000 years of history and, remarkably, is still going strong. Thanks to the Great Jubilee celebrations in 2000, many of the buildings were renovated, polished and cleaned. Classical Rome, Medieval Rome and Baroque Rome all received attention as the pollution and decay of decades, even centuries, was carefully buffed away. The Italian capital is, today, simply one of the best-preserved and most beautifully historic cities in the world and, with new anti-pollution measures, will hopefully remain as such for centuries to come. It is a vibrant metropolis sprawling over not just its famed seven hills, but gradually extending beyond them into the valleys of the **Roma Campagna**.

Rome is the elegant capital of a nation of over 58 million people, its seat of parliament, a major year-round tourist destination, and the city is also the hub of the Italian cinema and television industry. And within its ancient city confines lies one of the world's smallest independent states, La Città del Vaticano, the Vatican City, home of the Catholic Church and the Pope. It is the final destination for millions of pilgrims intent on visiting the world's largest basilica and, if luck permits, glimpsing their spiritual leader.

Together, Rome and the Vatican City offer the visitor an opportunity to voyage into the past, to marvel at exquisite art and architecture, to sample another vibrant culture, and to be seduced by that exuberant *gioia di vivere* which permeates the Italian capital.

Top Attractions

*** Roman Forum and **Colosseum:** the pulse of Ancient Rome.
*** St Peter's and the **Vatican Museums:** some of Christendom's magnificent artistic achievements.
** The Pantheon: a beautiful place of worship from Imperial times.
** Campidoglio and the **Capitoline Museums:** Michelangelo's harmonious square now sheltering an irreplaceable collection of Greek and Italian artefacts.
* Campo de' Fiori: a colourful morning market.

◄ *Opposite: One of Rome's most appealing flower stalls, in Piazza di Spagna.*

FACT FILE

- **Population of Italy:** 60.2 million
- **Population of the city of Rome:** 2.7 million
- **Size of country:** 301,270km² (117,684 sq miles)
- **Coastline:** 7600km (4750 miles)
- **Religion:** 98 per cent Catholic
- **River Tiber** (*Il Tevere*): 405km (252 miles) in length
- **Principal revenues:** manufacturing, tourism, textiles, agricultural products (wine) and automobile industry
- Rome is divided into 35 political *quartieri* (including Ostia) and 6 **suburbs** (including EUR, which has a special status).

▼ *Below: The River Tiber meanders through Rome, bringing a welcome breath of fresh air to an often rather congested city.*

THE LAND

Consisting of just over 300,000km² (115,800 sq miles) of boot-shaped land, stretching 1300km (808 miles) from the snowy heights of Mont Blanc (4810m/15,782ft), through the long, mountainous backbone of the **Apennines**, to the Sicilian Isola di Luce, or Island of Light, Italy has an impressive variety of topographical features and climates. Rome lies some 570km (355 miles) from Milan, and 219km (136 miles) from Naples, the second- and third-largest cities respectively. While the **River Po** is the country's longest river – at 652km (405 miles) – the **Tevere**, or **River Tiber**, is the second longest (405km/252 miles) and rises in the Apennines, flowing through Rome and out to sea at Ostia, 24km (15 miles) southwest of Rome. Although the capital was built on seven 'hills', they are really little more than hillocks and Rome is essentially a flat city on a flat, alluvial plain.

Beyond this, the land rises to a landscape of volcanic mountains and crater lakes – the **Roman Campagna**, or countryside, much beloved by artists, writers and today's tourists. To the south are the **Colli Albani** (the Alban Hills) and the **Castelli Romani**, a series of fortresses, each occupying a strategically elevated position above what was once a crater and is now, more often than not, a lake.

The Tiber

Il Tevere, as the Tiber is known in Italian, snakes through Rome, from north to south, separating the western suburbs, the Vatican and Trastevere from the remains of Ancient Rome and the suburbs that run from north, through east and south of the city. The Tiber has some paved banks but, for the most part, it plays little part in either the recreation or commerce of the city. In its midst, between **Trastevere** and the Ghetto, it has formed a small island, **Isola Tiberina**, known for its hospitals. Fourteen bridges span the river within the city walls, among which are the pedestrian bridges of **Ponte Sisto** (commissioned by Pope Sixtus IV), the **Ponte Sant'Angelo**, and Rome's oldest standing bridge, the **Ponte Fabricio**, built in 62BC.

▲ *Above: Piazza della Trinità dei Monti affords fine views over Rome.*

The Neighbourhoods

The city is divided into a score of political divisions, but the parts are more frequently referred to by the **neighbourhoods** such as those of Campo de' Fiori, Piazza Navona, Colosseum or San Giovanni in Laterano, and most of these neighbourhoods often have their own identities. **Campo de' Fiori**, for instance, attracts young, somewhat bohemian tenants for whom the myriad cafés and markets in the area provide informal meeting points. **Piazza Navona**, with its stately palaces, is a popular residential neighbourhood. Here, too, are scores of restaurants and cafés, not only in the elegant piazza but also in the tiny alleys and cobbled streets leading away from the piazza. Behind the **Colosseum**, and extending towards **San Giovanni** in Laterano, is a pleasant residential area with a large

ANGELS AND DEMONS

Stepping into the pages of Dan Brown's bestsellers, you are guided on a walking tour of parts of the city, solving puzzles and learning about the enigmas which Brown touched on in his books. Alternatively the same company (www.angels anddemons.it) will walk you around central Rome at night. Both are fabulous experiences and very popular. Take good walking shoes!

▲ *Above: With the first rays of spring sunshine, Rome's restaurants spill onto the pavements.*
▶ *Opposite: The Giardini Pincio are a favourite playground for the young.*

hospital. Life here is less stressed but it's only a bus ride from the centre. **Piazza di Spagna** is an address for well-heeled citizens and, although the apartments are of all sizes, the rents are exceptionally high. Streets are cleaned regularly and decorated with flowers, and the residents dress with some elegance.

Santa Maria Maggiore, one of the great basilicas in Rome, is now surrounded by many Asian and African homes: the **market** in **Piazza Vittorio Emanuele** offers (nearly) as many exotic fruits and vegetables as it does Italian ones. The restaurants in this neighbourhood reflect the foreign influence. So too, the area around **Stazione di Termini** which, although at first glance may not be appealing, is a multi-ethnic neighbourhood with some interesting restaurants. This area backs onto **San Lorenzo**, a typical student area catering for the University that is located here.

Trastevere is unique. Across the river, devoid of spectacular ancient monuments, life pulsates in quaint narrow, cobbled streets as it has done for centuries – and that makes it one of the most traditional neighbourhoods in Rome. Trastevere attracts foreigners, students, lovers of Rome and, above all, lovers of Italian cuisine.

HILLS OF ROME

Often quoted in literature, the seven hills of Rome are: **Avertine**, **Capitoline**, **Celian** (or **Coelian**), **Esquiline**, **Palatine**, **Quirinale** and the **Viminale**.

Climate

Rome enjoys a Mediterranean climate. Its summers are hot and dry – July daytime temperatures are often around 30°C (86°F). In June and September, temperatures average 27°C (81°F) and June is by far the sunniest month of the year. The night temperatures are a little lower, and in both June and September can warrant a light jacket or pullover. Rainfall is minimal in July (less than 10mm, or under half an inch), but can be slightly more during August when precipitation takes the form of thunderstorms: short, sharp rainfall. In June, rainfall averages some 20mm (still less than an inch), while September is liable to have more rain, up to 60mm (2 inches). Romans say that the autumn weather in October is glorious. The days are pleasantly warm, averaging 22°C (72°F), and nights are cool, but the hours of light are already shorter.

The winter months can, however, also be very pleasant. Temperatures from mid-November through March average around 13°C (56°F) in the day, but drop to 5–7°C (41–45°F) at night. November also sees the most rainfall, with almost 95mm (nearly 4 inches) and the rainfall continues, though decreasingly, through the following months. April is spring, and it is usually warm enough to eat out at midday. Temperatures average 18°C (65°F) during the day, but can drop again at night. Rainfall in April is around 40mm (1.5 inches). May can be a marvellous time to visit. The vegetation is lush, temperatures average 23°C (74°F), days are long, and rainfall is slightly less than in April.

PUBLIC HOLIDAYS

Capo d'Anno
(New Year's Day)
Epifania
(Epiphany or 12th Night)
Lunedì di Pasqua
(Easter Monday)
Giorno della Liberazione
(Liberation Day: 25 April)
Primo Maggio/Giorno di Lavoro (Labour Day: 1 May)
Festa de la Repubblica
(Republic Day: 2 June)
SS Pietro e Paolo (St Peter and St Paul's Day: 29 June)
Ferragosto (Assumption of the Virgin: 15 August)
Ognissanti (All Saints Day: 1 November)
Immacolata Concezione
(Immaculate Conception: 8 December)
Natale (Christmas Day: 25 December)
Santo Stefano (St Stephen's or Boxing Day: 26 December)

Romans, like Italians in general, adore sport. After all, they hosted the 1960 Olympic Games and the 1990 World Cup. But they prefer to talk about it rather than to swap their designer wear for shirts and shorts. The result is that the precious few facilities that exist in the capital are almost exclusively for members. However, if you are a jogger, you can join the legions in **Villa Borghese**, the **Pincio Gardens** of the **Villa Doria Pamphilj**, many of whom run the dog at the same time. Serious runners can enter the **annual marathon** (late March). **Cycling** enthusiasts might want to plan a visit to coincide with the **Giro de Lazio** (June) or the **Giro d'Italia** (May/June) which sometimes passes through Rome. Close to many a Roman heart is the performance of either **Lazio** or **Roma**, the capital's two world-class **soccer** clubs. Games are held most weekends at the **Stadio Olimpico**.

The Wild Side of Rome

In the heart of a European metropolis, you would not expect to find much wildlife but greater Rome boasts over 1300 species of flora and 145 species of fauna. In addition to these, villas and public gardens are planted with indigenous and exotic trees and flowers, tended by the municipality. The most noticeable wild inhabitants of the city are the myriad **cats** (many of which are now entirely feral), which have the run of Rome's Classical ruins. The cats are protected by law, and the authorities regularly run counts and controls. In the many parks and protected areas (most are not in the Classical heart of the city but are easily accessible by public transport), the **bird** population thrives. One of the best places to enjoy the city's varied flora and fauna is the **Orto Botanico** (under university auspices) where **feeding points** and **nesting boxes** encourage visits by, amongst others, owls, woodpeckers, flycatchers, goldfinches and tits. Other excellent areas for contact with nature include **Villa Ada** – with its plantations of cedar, pines, oaks and metasequoias – the wooded areas and formal gardens of the **Villa Doria Pamphilj** and, in the heart of Rome, the parkland around **Villa Borghese** (now the **Museo Borghese**) and the various areas of formal gardens. The latter include the **Giardini Segreti** (Secret Gardens), the **Viale delle Magnolie** (the Avenue of the Magnolias), and the **Giardino del Lago** (the Lake Garden), with its attractive reflections.

HISTORY IN BRIEF

Rome's importance in world history is due to its unique position as the centre of the **Roman Empire** and of **Western Christianity**. The Roman Empire and the papacy have fashioned not just the fabric of Rome, but the geography and civilization of most of Europe. In the case of the Catholic Church, its influence has shaped societies throughout the world.

▲ *Above: A representation of Romulus and Remus, Rome's founders, stands behind the Campidoglio.*
◀ *Opposite: Protected by law, the feral cats of Rome have the run of the Colosseum.*

The Founding of Rome

Archaeological excavations have confirmed the existence of **Etruscan** and **Sabine** settlements on the hills around Rome towards the middle of the 8th century BC. According to tradition, the history of Rome starts with the twins, **Romulus** and **Remus** (*see panel, page 33*), and the founding of Rome in 753BC, a legend propagated by the historian **Livy**, writing in the 1st century BC. After the time of Romulus, Rome was ruled by a succession of seven kings (mostly Etruscan) until **Tarquinius Superbus** was driven out in 509BC.

The Republic

Rome subsequently became a Republic and two consuls were elected to rule the populace. Besides the fact that the Romans gradually began enlarging their stronghold, they also exercised influence outside their own geographical area and, by the 3rd century BC, most of Italy fell under Rome's command – an extraordinary feat when considering the power of rival city-states (Carthage, Athens or Alexandria) and the means at their disposal. Roman society was divided into three broad groups: the **patricians**, descendants of Rome's original families who had the right to vote in the Senate; the **plebians**, ordinary folk, including freed slaves; and **slaves**, who had the minimum of rights.

ETRUSCAN ART

The Etruscans (who invaded in 616BC from what is today Tuscany) previously ruled a large area of Central Italy, including Rome, right up to the 6th century BC. Some of the oldest artistic remains in the city are the wonderful Etruscan items on display in either the **Vatican Galleries** or **Villa Giulia**, and the bronze sculpture of a she-wolf suckling Romulus and Remus in the **Capitoline Museums**. Among the exhibits to be seen are bronze and terracotta pieces retrieved from burial chambers north of Rome.

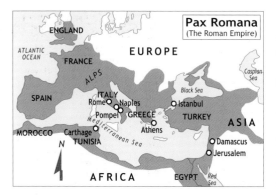

Pax Romana
(The Roman Empire)

The demands of an ever-expanding Roman society became critical: more slaves were required, supplies of grain and food produce were insufficient, and increasing reserves of metal were needed. The solution was to send out the **legions**, well-trained and highly disciplined soldiers, to conquer productive distant territories and incorporate them into the republic. From the 3rd century BC, the Republic extended so relentlessly that it soon comprised all the territory from Spain to Syria, and from southern France to the north of Africa.

In 49BC, the famous military commander, **Gaius Julius Caesar**, crossed the Rubicon River and challenged control of the Republic. He seized power and, in 44BC, unconstitutionally declared himself Emperor. He was, however, assassinated in Rome a month later.

The Empire

On Caesar's death, Rome was thrust into civil war, which ended in 27BC when Octavian, assuming the name of **Augustus**, became the first elected emperor.

Augustus was one of Rome's greatest emperors and, for 41 years, the citizens lived in peace and thrived. It was the golden age of literature, when **Livy**, **Ovid**, **Horace** and **Virgil** wrote works that are still read and appreciated today. Augustus applied rules of civic building and did much to beautify the city, leaving a report when he died in AD14 in which he stated, 'I was born to a city of brick and left a city of marble.'

Then, in the middle of the rule of Augustus, a child was born in one of the most eastern provinces of the Roman Empire. Albeit indirectly, **Jesus of Nazareth** was to change a great part of the Western world, including Ancient Rome.

PAX ROMANA

In its heyday, at the death of **Emperor Hadrian** (AD117), the Roman Empire extended from today's Portugal to Damascus, and from Northumberland in northern England to the Nile in Egypt. It covered about 40 provinces (and touched on, by today's geography, some 40 different countries). Around 50 million people of many different races and religions lived in the vast Empire, a territory that embraced some half a dozen climatic zones. The conquered were absorbed into the Empire, made *cives Romani* (citizens of Rome) and, in some cases, rose to the enviable position of Emperor. Notable among these were **Trajan** and **Hadrian** (both from Spain) and **Septimius Severus** (from north Africa).

Augustus was followed by a line of emperors of varying competence and sanity (including **Tiberius**, **Caligula** and **Nero**) until the Hispanic citizen, **Trajan**, took charge in AD98, and his successor, **Hadrian**, reinforced the position of the Empire. Rome was at its height during this period: its territories comprised 40 provinces (part of 40 countries today), it had over 84,800km (53,000 miles) of paved roads, and was home to some 50 million people.

When Hadrian died in AD138, the Empire was never to attain such geographical or political prestige again. Society degenerated into excess and discipline no longer glued together the fabric of the Empire. Revenues that should have filled Rome's coffers were pilfered; the provinces did business with each other and the capital's fortunes foundered. Under **Diocletian** (AD285–305), the Empire was divided into East and West, weakening rather than consolidating its political clout.

In AD306, **Constantine** became Emperor of an obviously declining Rome. He legalized Christianity in AD313 with the Edict of Milan and established a shrine at the place of St Peter's tomb. In AD330, Constantine moved the capital of the Eastern Empire to **Constantinople** (named, naturally, after himself), today's Istanbul. On his deathbed, he was baptized, becoming the first Christian emperor.

In the following two centuries, forces from the north of Europe made their presence felt not only in Spain and France, but also in the boot-shaped peninsula. **Attila the Hun** sacked much of Italy while the **Vandals** took Spain. In AD476, **Odoacar**, king of the Goths, deposed Emperor Romulus Augustulus, bringing an end to the Western Empire.

The Dark Ages and Medieval Rome

The last centuries of the first millennium were dark years for Rome. Revenues dropped and its population declined, yet Christianity thrived. The Lombards in the north proved increasingly powerful and menaced Rome,

> **MUCH-MALIGNED NERO**
>
> Contrary to popular belief, Nero did not actually fiddle while Rome burned. He was in Ostia, 24km (15 miles) away and, knowing that the tenements by the Tiber were doomed, turned his attentions to writing a new **fire code** and planning a new city. He began construction the day after the nine-day fire burned out. Nero was instrumental in building **aqueducts** to bring water to Rome and he reinforced the city's water supply so that the scale of such a disaster would be reduced if fire was to break out again.

▼ *Below: A distinguished and fair ruler, Hadrian took the Empire to its largest extent.*

ROME'S OLDEST RESTAURANT

Dating back to 1528, **La Campana**, at Vicolo della Campana 18, tel: 06 687 5273, is the city's oldest and one of its favourite dining spots. Celebrated guests who have feasted here on its traditional *cucina Romana* include **Goethe**, **Picasso** and **Pasolini**. Dishes to sample include its *abacchio al forno* (roast lamb) and *cervello ai carciofi* (brains in artichokes). The artichoke ravioli are also superb, as are the courgette (squash/zucchini) flowers stuffed with anchovies and mozzarella. Fish dishes are also very popular.

where the popes held sway over the **Catholic Church**, and conflict between political power and the power of the papacy became commonplace. However, Pope Leo III crowned **Charlemagne**, the Frankish king, **Holy Roman Emperor** in AD800 as a reward for ousting the Lombards. Little more than an honorary title at first, the Holy Roman Empire became the focus of constant strife between rival claims of successive popes and emperors. Struggles arose and were resolved, but the rivalry continued to simmer well into the 13th century. On the death of Innocent III in 1216, the papacy and papal possessions were at their height, while the Empire's sway declined and the popes lived in a fashion that was far from ascetic.

In 1309, the French-born popes went into exile at Avignon. In 1377, the papacy officially returned to Rome, but Urban VI was so unpopular that an 'anti-pope' was elected in Avignon. The Great Western Schism split the world for a further 39 years, with a third pope being elected in 1409 by a council in Pisa. Eventually, in 1417, all three were sacked and Martin V, a pope of Roman origin, was elected. The breach was healed and the Vatican became the only papal residence.

▼ *Below: The Baroque chapel by Carlo Maderno in Santa Maria sopra Minerva.*

◄ *Left: For Catholic visitors, lay or religious, the Vatican is the most important sight.*

Renaissance and Baroque

At the beginning of the 1500s, Catholicism was further challenged from the north as **Martin Luther** gained support and the Church irrevocably separated into two organizations with distinctly different doctrines. The papacy spearheaded the **Counter-Reformation** and shored up the Catholic faith against the threat of religious reform. When Pope Julius II came to the power in 1503, Rome's appearance began to change for the better. Nicholas V had ordered the demolition of the old St Peter's and Julius II began the new **St Peter's**, which was to take 120 years to complete. In 1527, however, Rome was sacked by the Holy Roman Emperor Charles V and many of its artistic treasures were lost – but the power of the city's elite continued. The Jesuit Order was founded by the Spaniard **St Ignatius Loyola** in 1537 and a number of elaborately decorated churches were built to house the new order. Thanks to many of the enlightened aristocracy who assumed the papacy through the 16th and 17th centuries – the **Renaissance** and the **Baroque** periods of art – Rome recaptured some of its former architectural glory, and many of the city's elegant bridges, fountains, churches, convents and patrician palazzi date from these two centuries. By the mid-17th century, the economic power of the country lay in the hands of northern Italy. Papal territories and influence gradually diminished to the extent that Rome's political role in the 18th century was more or less negligible.

▲ *Above: The monument to Vittorio Emanuele II looks as good as it did when unveiled in 1911.*

The 19th Century

In 1798, **Napoleon** captured Rome and declared it a republic. Some 10 years later, between 1809 and 1811, the French annexed the papal states, turning Rome into the second capital of the French empire, seat of the king of Rome, Napoleon's son.

Following Napoleon's downfall in 1815, Rome and the papal states were restored to the Pope, but a home-grown desire for Italian unification – known as the **Risorgimento** – arose, fostered by secret societies such as the **Carbonari** and **Young Italy**. In 1848, political unrest swept through the whole Italian peninsula and **Giuseppe Garibaldi** (*see* panel, page 101) established a short-lived Roman republic the following year. The Pope fled but was reinstated by the French and Garibaldi

HISTORICAL CALENDAR

753BC According to legend, twin brothers Romulus and Remus founded Rome.
700BC Rise of Etruscan Empire.
509BC Rome becomes a republic.
390BC Gauls invade Italy.
264–41BC First Punic War.
133BC Romans invade and occupy Spain.
44BC Julius Caesar assumes supreme power, but is assassinated just one month later.
27BC Augustus becomes the first Emperor.
AD54 Nero becomes Emperor.
313 Emperor Constantine proclaims freedom of worship.
476 The end of the Western Roman Empire.
800 Charlemagne proclaimed Holy Roman Emperor.
1309–77 The popes go into exile at Avignon.
1527 King Charles V's troops sack Rome.

1798 Napoleon I declares Rome a republic.
1861 Italy united and Turin becomes capital.
1871 Rome proclaimed capital city.
1922 Mussolini assumes power.
1940 Italy enters World War II.
1946 Italy is again declared a republic.
1957 Treaty of Rome signed, founding the European Union.
1960 Rome hosts Olympics.
1978 Aldo Moro kidnapped and assassinated.
1990 Rome hosts the soccer World Cup.
2000 Catholicism's Great Jubilee.
2005 Death of Pope John Paul II and election of German Pope Benedict XVI.
2011 Beatification of Pope John Paul II.

returned to exile. Ten years later, Garibaldi supported the unification of Italy under the House of Piedmont, and his successful conquest of Sicily and Naples in 1860 – with his 1000 followers, his Brazilian wife, Anita, and their dog – enabled southern Italy to be united with the north under king **Victor Emmanuel II**. Unification was completed by the annexation of Venice in 1866 and then the papal states in 1870. In 1871, Rome finally became the capital of a united Italy.

The 20th Century and Beyond

In 1922, the fascist leader, **Benito Mussolini**, marched on Rome and assumed power. He orchestrated the 1929 signing of the **Lateran Treaty**, finally establishing peace between the government and the papacy. Papal jurisdiction was confined to the Vatican City and a few extra-territorial possessions, but the Church was given a vast sum of money in compensation and became a strong ally of the State.

Mussolini took Italy into World War II in 1940, but was executed in 1945 while trying to flee to Switzerland. At the end of the War, **Victor Emmanuel III** abdicated and although Umberto II took the throne, he lasted only until the following year when the Republic was re-proclaimed by a popular referendum. Umberto II and his family were exiled and took up residence in Switzerland. In 1957, Italy became one of the six founder members of the European Common Market – now the 27-strong European Union – by signing the **Treaty of Rome**.

The staging of the **Olympic Games** in 1960 was the highlight of a decade that deteriorated during the 1970s into political strife and terrorism

BENITO MUSSOLINI (1883–1943)

Mussolini founded the Fascist Movement in 1919 and by 1924 held the majority of power in Italy. To garner lacking papal support, he signed the **Lateran Treaty** in 1929, then, in the 1930s (during the Spanish Civil War), aligned his party with **Franco**. In 1935, he invaded Ethiopia and, siding with Hitler, took Italy into World War II in 1940. Not all Italy was pro-Fascist and Mussolini executed many of those who turned against him, including his son-in-law. In 1943, **Il Duce** (as he was known) was deposed from within his party and interned in the **Abruzzi** only to be liberated by the Germans. On flight to neutral Switzerland after the Germans surrendered in 1945, he and his mistress, **Clara Petacci**, were lynched.

▼ Below: From most parts of Rome, the dome of St Peter's Basilica is visible.

ROMAN REVENUES

Until the 1970s, Rome relied on **tourism** and **agriculture** as its main sources of income. In the last quarter of the 20th century, however, it developed a whole new range of industries. The most lucrative are **mechanical construction**, **aeronautics** as well as **motorbike** and **scooter** manufacture. Its **electronics** industry has expanded, while refineries for both **chemicals** and **petroleum** have been built near Fiumicino. It also has an increasing **paper manufacturing** and **printing** sector.

▼ *Below: The Vatican's elite Swiss Guards date back to the 16th century.*

attacks, which included the assassination of prime minister, Aldo Moro, by the **Red Brigade** in 1978. In the same year, **John Paul II** became the first non-Italian pope to be elected since 1522. He was responsible for organizing the Church's 2000-year anniversary in 2000. After battling ill health for years, he died in 2005 and was succeeded by a German, who took the name of **Pope Benedict XVI**.

GOVERNMENT AND ECONOMY

Italy is a republic, with the president a ceremonial head of state holding office for a seven-year term. The current incumbent is **Giorgio Napolitano** who assumed office in 2006. **Silvio Berlusconi**, Italy's controversial billionaire, was voted in for a third time as Prime Minister in April 2008.

Despite being politically united for over 100 years, there remains in Italy a substantial north–south divide. The north of the country, and particularly Milan, accounts for only 25 per cent of the country in size and population, but is responsible for over 70 per cent of the gross domestic product (GDP). The Mezzogiorno, or south of the country, has a large population but is not as productive. Rome sits, more or less, on the divide and while it has its fair share of small industries, it is tourism in particular that brings revenue to the capital.

In terms of GDP, Italy ranks eighth in the world (just behind France and Great Britain) and although it has some mineral resources (notably natural gas), much of the country's revenue derives from its **manufacturing industries**, in particular its mechanical engineering, iron and steel works, chemical industry, agro-

alimentary production, car manufacturing, and its all-important textile industry, which ranks fourth in world production. The country ranks second (behind France) for volume of **wine** produced, and also second in olive production. It is, however, Europe's largest **rice** producer (the area around the Po in northern Italy is the main rice-producing region). Despite having a coastline of over 7600km (4720 miles) long, fishing does not contribute a great deal to the GDP.

▲ *Above: The unwinding spiral of the Vatican's beautiful double staircase.*

La Città del Vaticano (Vatican City)
The Head of State not only of the Vatican City but also of the Catholic Church worldwide, the **Pope** has absolute power in the Vatican. A **governor** is responsible for the administrative, judicial and economic services of the State. The Vatican City has a surface area of less than one square kilometre and a population of around 1000 people, swelled by the 2000 people who live outside but work within this tax-free state. Revenues are gathered from tourism, pilgrimages and donations, enabling the Vatican to return a well-balanced account sheet each year. Revenues from tourism include the entrance fees to its **museums**, a wide range of **religious souvenirs** and its **unique stamps**.

WINE PRODUCTION

Italy is the world's largest producer of wine, and the industry is still growing. Small wine holdings proliferate, the number of DOC areas (**Denominazione d'Origine Controlata**, the system for categorizing wine by area and ensuring quality) has increased and more attention is being given to producing high-quality wines than the traditional *vino di tavola* (table wines). Indeed, the finest red wines compete with the best in the world, but they are pricing themselves out of the ordinary wine-drinkers' market. However, wine lovers are now watching the so-called 'emerging regions', the newer DOCs in the east of Italy.

INTRODUCING ROME AND THE VATICAN

THE PEOPLE

Italians are generally gregarious, excitable and passionate. They can laugh and cry in the same breath, shout one minute and fall in the arms of their adversary the next. They are noisy, musical and willingly trade work for pleasure. Hedonists to the last, they will sacrifice much for the opportunity to dine and chat. In the last few decades, Rome has absorbed African and Asian immigrants and in some neighbourhoods the demographics have changed radically. The Italian spirit remains nevertheless enduring and those traditions, which attract the new resident or tourist to the country, are still upheld.

Language

Latin, as spoken in Ancient Rome, has defined not only modern Italian but some six other languages too, and has given us our alphabet and structured English grammar. The Italian spoken today is marvellously similar (at least to linguists!) to the language spoken 2000 years ago. In the 3rd century AD, publishers evolved the lower case (previously, texts were written in capital letters only), and in Medieval times the 'I' was elevated into a 'J' and 'V' split into 'U', 'V' and 'W'. As a result of World War II and the increasing Americanization of Europe, the language has embraced some modernisms, an evolving slang and a general loosening of the once-stringent Latin grammar. With its copious vowels, modern Italian is a melodious language – and one that lends itself well to verse and song. As with all the regions in Italy, Rome has evolved its own dialect and slang. Italian speakers will notice that Romans hardly pronounce the ends of their words – a habit frowned upon further north in Florence where the language is considered at its purest. Travellers who make the effort

LANGUAGE SCHOOLS

When in Rome... why not learn Italian? Three of the most respected language schools in town are:
• **Dante Alighieri**, piazza Bologna 1, tel: 06 4423 1400, www.clidante.it Old, established school offering language and cultural courses for all levels.
• **Berlitz**, via Virgilio 8, tel: 06 687 2561, www.berlitz.it This school offers courses for all abilities and needs.
• **Scuola Leonardo da Vinci**, piazza dell'Orologio 7, tel: 06 6889 2513, www.scuola leonardo.com Present in Italy's major cities, another good option for learning Italian at all levels.
• **International House**, via Marghera 22, tel: 06 446 2592, www.dilit.it Known usually for its English courses, it offers excellent Italian and other culturally interesting courses.

to learn some basic Italian will be met with warmth and enthusiasm, but those who don't, will no doubt find that their Roman hosts are quite competent in English!

Religion

Some 98 per cent of Italians are **Catholic**, but Rome also has a small percentage of **Jews**, **Protestants** and **Muslims**, the latter reflecting the recent immigration trends. Those visitors who would like to see the Pope should apply to the Prefetto della Casa Pontificia, Città del Vaticano, 00120 Rome, fax: 06 6988 5863 (www.vatican.va) to attend the Wednesday Papal Audiences. Apply ahead of time in writing, or the Monday beforehand in person at the office to the right of St Peter's.

Catholics celebrate all the traditional religious holidays, with particular reverence to **Christmas** and **Easter**. Unlike some other Italian towns, Rome has few festivals. However, if you are in town on **Good Friday**, the Pope leads a night-time procession of the cross at the Colosseum, and on **Easter Sunday** he addresses the thousands who gather on **St Peter's Square**. The **Festa di San Pietro** (29 June) honours St Peter, Rome's patron saint, while the 10 days before and after **Christmas** are filled with festive gaiety.

◄◄ *Opposite: Traffic police need to be particularly vigilant in congested central Rome.*
◄ *Left: Rome's beautiful churches host a continual stream of weddings every Saturday during the warm summer months.*

ARTISTS AND ARCHITECTS

- **Gianlorenzo Bernini** (sculptor and architect) 1598–1680
- **Francesco Borromini** (architect) 1599–1667
- **Donato Bramante** (painter and architect) 1444–1514
- **Michelangelo Buonarotti** (painter, sculptor and architect) 1475–1564
- **Michelangelo Merisi da Caravaggio** (painter) 1571–1610
- **Annibale Carracci** (painter) 1560–1609
- **Pietro da Cortona** (painter and architect) 1596–1669
- **Giacomo della Porta** (architect) 1553–1602
- **Carlo Maderno** (architect) 1556–1629
- **Guido Reni** (painter) 1575–1642
- **Raffaello (Raphael) Sanzio** (painter and architect) 1483–1520
- **Giacomo Vignola** (architect) 1507–1573

Art and Architecture

Rome breathes history and art. No single civilization in Europe has left such an enduring mark on their lands and the civilizations that followed. Wherever you wander within the city walls, modern Rome juxtaposes with the ancient city: a crumbling wall or Corinthian column might easily be incorporated into a 21st-century steel-and-glass office; an 1800-year-old flight of foot-worn steps may now be used by high-heeled clientele. The successive generations of builders – from the Ancient Romans onwards – have filched both building material and works of art, shamelessly incorporating them in new constructions.

In Rome's 2700 years of history, it has witnessed two truly great artistic periods interspersed with other magnificent achievements. The first period peaked with the height of the **Roman Empire**, around AD138, and the second was the **Baroque** age, an era that consciously chose to embellish the Classical harmony which preceding Renaissance artists had sought so hard to achieve. Imperial Rome was the age of expansion, and was witness to an intense building programme, both civic and domestic. It was also the era of short reigns – and each emperor wanted monuments to immortalize his own particular achievements. In addition to the

◄ *Left: Detail from a Roman sarcophagus, Vatican Museums.*
◄◄ *Opposite: Part of a Roman mosaic, in the Palazzo Massimo, showing hippos.*

* **Museo Nazionale delle Paste Alimentari** (National Museum of Pasta), piazza Scanderberg 117, tel: 06 699 1120, www.museodella pasta.it Near the Trevi fountain, all you ever wanted to know about pasta.
* **Museo Tipologico Nazionale del Presepio** (National Museum of Nativity Scenes), via Tor de'Conti 31a, tel: 06 679 6146, www.presepio.it A large collection of items from nativity crèches and statuettes from many different countries.
* **Museo Internazionale del Cinema e dello Spettacolo** (International Museum of Cinema and Entertainment), via Portuense 101, tel: 06 390 0266, www.museo delcinema.it Film-making equipment, film library and a vast photographic library. Booking required.
* **Piccolo Museo delle Anime del Purgatorio** (Museum of the Souls in Purgatory), Chiesa del Sacro Cuore del Suffragio, Lungotevere Prati 12, tel: 06 6880 6517. Traces of fire left on cloths, wood tablets and breviaries by souls in Purgatory.

architectural legacy, which includes the remains of various **Fora**, the **Colosseum**, **Ara Pacis**, the triumphal arches, the **Baths of Diocletian** or **Caracalla**, and the **Pantheon**, there are fabulous mosaics, frescoes and countless breathtaking sculptures of Roman men and women, so lifelike you can almost believe you passed them on the street just minutes earlier.

The Rome of the early Christians is harder to discover, for much of the city has been rebuilt on old buildings. What remains of this epoch, however, are the numerous floor **mosaics**, the **catacombs** and the inscribed fragment from the **True Cross** in Santa Croce in Gerusalemme. From early Medieval days, there is **Santa Maria sopra Minerva**, the only extant Gothic church in Rome, and the beautiful apse mosaics in **Santa Maria** in **Trastevere** and **Santa Maria Maggiore**.

When the popes returned from exile in Avignon in 1378, they did much to redress the importance of the city. It was, once again, a time of concerted building programmes and a renewed interest in the arts. The building of St Peter's was begun, and Sixtus IV commissioned the **Sistine Chapel**, decorated later by **Michelangelo** under Pope Julius II, who also enlarged the Vatican Palace. Paul III endorsed Michelangelo's designs for **St Peter's**, the **Campidoglio** and **Palazzo Farnese**. Not only were the

▲ *Above: Despite the rain, filming continues in the Campo de' Fiori.*
▶ *Opposite: A tribute to writer Byron, in the Villa Borghese.*

popes prolific patrons but so too their cardinals; many of these individuals built lavish palaces and commissioned works of art for themselves and their families.

Baroque reached its purest form in Rome. This was an era of great religious architecture and, in the face of Protestantism, a move to make Catholicism more attractive through an appeal to the spectator's emotions. The greatest exponents of the Baroque were **Gianlorenzo Bernini** and his great rival, **Francesco Borromini**. Post-Baroque Rome is not devoid of buildings, but there is little of outstanding merit. Of interest are the vast monument to **Victor Emmanuel II**, the Foro Italico (a sports centre built under Mussolini), buildings of EUR and some of Pier Luigi Nervi's work for the 1960 Olympics.

Film

In 1935 the large Rome film studios, **Cinecittà**, were founded to give an élan to the increasingly popular film industry. This was the beginning of neorealism, with such young film-makers as **Rossellini**, **De Sica** and **De Santis**. A number of the darker landmarks of 20th-century cinema came out of Italy – Rossellini's *Roma Città Aperta* and De Sica's *Ladri di Bicicletta*, for instance. Such was the success of Cinecittà that, for a while, the studios were courted by an international coterie of film makers, and the epics *Ben Hur* and *Spartacus* were both made here before the indulgent, heady days of the 1960s left an entirely different legacy on celluloid. **Federico Fellini**

FEDERICO FELLINI (1920–93)

One of Italy's foremost film directors, Fellini was born in **Rimini**, on the east coast of Italy. He soon gravitated to Rome and collaborated on the film scripts of a number of lesser movies. He made his first film, *Luci del Varietà* in 1950 and, during the course of his life, wrote and directed 24 films. Amongst these were the classics, *La Strada* (1954), *La Dolce Vita* (1959), *Otto e Mezzo* (1963) and *Satyricon* (1969), all of which had a profound effect on Italian cinema. His later works never received the same acclaim as these early films. His last film was produced in 1990 and he died in Rome in 1993.

made the unforgettable *La Dolce Vita* in 1969 (with Anita Ekberg wading through the Fontana di Trevi) and later, *Otto e Mezzo* and *Satyricon*. **Lucchino Visconti** co-produced the classic *Il Gattopardo* as well as the beautifully filmed *Morte a Venezia* in 1969. In the 1970s, the political directors left their mark. **Bernardo Bertolucci** and **Pier Paolo Pasolini** became household names, but had to fight against a rising television industry to pull in cinema audiences. A few great films were made in the 1980s – notably *The Last Emperor* by Bertolucci and *Cinema Paradiso* by **Tornatore** – but the film studios were waning as the new breed of realism visualized by **Nanni Moretti** (*Caro Diario* was filmed around Rome) took hold. His success was only eclipsed by that of the runaway hit *La Vita è Bella* by **Roberto Benigni**. But perhaps Cinecittà's fortunes are improving. It is a popular centre for TV work and, extraordinarily, **Scorsese** filmed *Gangs of New York* here in 2001.

Music and Literature

Despite the wealth of visual arts, Rome has spawned few great musicians or writers – the exception being the Classical writers, **Ovid**, **Virgil** and **Horace** and, nearly 2000 years later, **Alberto Moravia**, a talented novelist. Rome has, however, influenced many and hosted even more artists, both Italian and foreign. The **Prix de Rome** was inaugurated in 1803, and many great artists and musicians – including **Poussin**, **Delacroix**, **Bizet** and **Debussy** – benefited from a study period at the French Academy in Villa Medici.

It was particularly fashionable to visit Rome in the 19th century – The Grand Tour of Europe's cultural heritage – and among the more notable to make Rome their temporary home were the English poets Keats, Byron and Shelley, and the American Henry James. Musicians who fell under the city's charms include Berlioz, Liszt and Puccini.

GREAT LATIN QUOTES

It took not just centuries, but nearly two millenia before any military dispatch usurped the brevity and wit with which **Julius Caesar** reported back from his historic success at the **Battle of Zela**: *Veni, vidi, vici*, he wrote ('I came, I saw, I conquered'). The other marvellous quote, sent by **Sir Charles Napier** in 1843, when the British were fighting to gain Sind province in northern India, was the telegram containing the single word *Peccavi*, which means 'I have sinned', and it thus punningly informed the British government of the successful expedition. The often-quoted phrase coined by the poet **Horace** was *Carpe diem* ('Seize the day'), which epitomizes a live-for-the-moment philosophy.

Food and Drink

Rome is not the culinary capital of Italy, but Romans certainly give cuisine its due importance. While breakfasts are rarely more than a strong *caffè* or frothy *cappuccino* and a feather-light flaky pastry in a convenient bar on the way to work, the *aperitivo*, lunch and dinner take on some importance. From April to the end of October, most restaurants with outdoor space will open their terraces or pavement seating, crowding tables and large umbrellas into their allotted space. It is usually a squeeze but this is part of the charm of dining *alfresco*.

Where to Eat

The tourist in Rome will find a bewildering variety of names for places to eat: each has its merits. At the bottom of the eateries is the humble *osteria*, an inexpensive hostelry, originally a place to stop for a meal or drink on a journey. Today's *osteria* might be nearer a wine bar in atmosphere, or it may offer a rustic atmosphere with good home cooking and fair prices. Slightly more up-market, the *trattoria* is a homely place (often entirely run by one family) with local cuisine. Some of Rome's best-loved *trattorie* are far from simple affairs and the prices reflect the quality of cuisine and a well-heeled clientele. An *enoteca*, another popular alternative, is the equivalent of a wine bar, complete with a fine selection of wines and snacks. If you want a quick bite without formality, a *tavola calda* is the answer. This delicatessen-type eatery offers plenty of ready-made dishes, usually sold by weight, which will be heated for you and can either be eaten on the premises or taken away. The ubiquitous *pizzeria* often serves more than just pizzas but the best

◀ Left: Lunch is a pleasure at an open-air trattoria.
◀◀ Opposite: Pasta is the base of every Italian's meal and in Rome the variety is endless.

GARIBALDI BISCUITS

A type of biscuit containing a layer of currants was much favoured by the Italian patriot Garibaldi, and named after him. Popular theory asserts that the currants represent the flies found in his rations when on campaign.

invariably come from a genuine *pizzeria* – wood fire, home-made dough and real mozzarella cheese. Alternatively, pre-cooked pizza slices are a great and economic snack for busy sightseers.

For a full meal, head for a *ristorante*; a *trattoria ristorante* will produce various local dishes, while a *ristorante* denotes a smarter locale with, perhaps, non-local dishes and pretensions to grandeur. Naturally, this also costs a bit more.

On the Menu

Roman restaurants are particularly good with *antipasti*. These cold dishes, varying from cooked vegetables to Parma ham, salamis and seafood, are presented on a trolley and are designed to whet the appetite before the *pasto*, or main meal, arrives.

Pasta (*see* panel, page 26) – sometimes coloured green, orange or mulberry and served with an imaginative range of sauces – usually constitutes the *primo piatto*, or first dish. **Rice**, too, is a favourite starter. *Risotto* (savoury rice dishes) include *risotto alla Romana*, with sweetbreads, liver and topped with slivers of cheese. *Bruschetta* are slices of bread rubbed with garlic and topped with chopped tomatoes and basil, which also make a good starter. **Bread** is always provided with a meal, but you pay for it – sometimes for each roll!

RESTAURANTS WITH A VIEW

Dinner among the rooftops of Rome? Reservations are advisable for these restaurants:
• **Roof Garden Restaurant and Bar** (Hotel Mediterraneo), tel: 06 488 4051.
• **La Pergola** (Hotel Hilton Cavalieri), tel: 06 3509 2152.
• **La Terrazza dei Papi** (Mercenate Palace Hotel), tel: 06 4470 2024.
• **Les Etoiles** (Hotel Atlante Star), tel: 06 687 3233.
• **Imàgo** (Hotel Hassler Villa Medici) tel: 06 69 9340.
• **Mirabelle**, via di Porta Pinciana 14, tel: 06 4216 8838.
• **L'Olimpo Roof Garden** (Hotel Bernini Bristol), tel: 06 4201 0469.
• **Minerva Roof Garden** (Grand Hotel de la Minerve), tel: 06 699 5201.

▲ *Above: There are many different types of breads, breadsticks and rolls.*
▶ *Opposite top: Gelateria in Piazza Navona.*
▶ *Opposite bottom: Apéritifs and cocktails are part of summer indulgences.*

DEPARTMENT STORES

Boutiques are still more frequent than department stores. However, for a good selection of clothing and household goods, head for the following: **La Rinascente**, Piazza Colonna, Via del Corso, Piazza Fiume and Via del Tritone; **Zara**, also at Galleria Sordi, via del Corso; **Upim**, via del Balduina 110; **Oviesse**, via Piazza V. Emanuele 108 or Viale Trastevere 62; the shopping centre at **Cinecittà Due** is also a good hunting ground. Lastly, **Discount dell' Alta Moda**, via Gesù e Maria 14–16 (near Piazza Popolo), is the place for Italian high-fashion bargains.

Secondi piatti, or **main courses**, to look out for are *abacchio*, tender roast lamb prepared in the oven and, when well cooked, falls off the bone; *vitello* (veal), which is offered as a scallop; a mouthwatering dish that includes Parma ham (known as *saltimbocca*), or is made with Marsala and sage. *Bifstecca* (steak) is usually cut fairly thin and grilled quickly to seal in the flavour. *Pollo* (chicken) will invariably feature on the menu: *Petto di Pollo* (chicken breast) is a popular and inexpensive dish, while *Pollo al Diavolo* (chicken in tomato and capsicum peppers) is often an excellent choice. Offal generally has less success with tourists than locals. Sweetbreads, *fegato* (liver) and *coda* (oxtail) are on most menus. There is plenty of fresh *pesce* (fish) available in Rome, but it is often the most expensive item on a menu. Usually grilled, the most popular include *rombo* (turbot), *baccalà* (cod), *spigola* (sea bass) and *sogliola* (sole). *Fritto misto* (mixed fried fish) can be delicious.

Do not expect **vegetables** with main dishes. There may be some French fries and perhaps a small garnish, but rarely more. *Contorni* (vegetables) are ordered separately. Favourites include *spinaci* (spinach), usually served with garlic and oil, or deep-fried chunks of *zucchini* (courgettes). An *insalata mista* (mixed salad), the most popular request, invariably incorporates lettuce-type leaves with *rucciola* (rocket) and tomato.

Don't miss out on the really excellent **cheeses** Italy produces. Apart from the well-known standards such as *parmigiano* (parmesan), *gorgonzola* or *bel paese*, try asking for *pecorino* (a hard cheese made of sheep's milk), *taleggio* (pungent, softish cheese) and *grana* (a cousin to *parmigiano*).

Romans are not really big on **desserts** but there is always a selection of *gelati* (ice cream) available for sale, or a delicious *tiramisù*, and sometimes you will be able to find a *crostata di ricotta* (a tasty local cheesecake). There is also a good selection of seasonal fruit, which marries well with cheese and is an excellent way to round off a meal.

What to Drink

In Italy, **wine** is considered an essential accompaniment to any meal. The nearest wine-producing region to Rome is the Castelli Romani district, which produces dry white wines. Look out for Frascati, Velletri and Grottaferrata, as many of the house wines offered in restaurants by the carafe come from here. Pinot Grigio (from the Veneto) and Vernaccia (from Tuscany) are also two light, white wines. The best red wines come from northern Italy, and the wines to look for here are the full-bodied rich Barolo, Barbaresco or Nebbiolo. Chianti is a popular, and sometimes excellent, wine from Tuscany. *Aqua minerale* (**mineral water**), either *frizzante* or *naturale*, is widely available. Ferrarelle, San Pellegrino and San Benedetto are popular varieties of sparkling water.

Italy also produces some very drinkable **beers**. Nastro Azzurro, Peroni and Moretti are among the most popular here, although internationally renowned beers are also widely available. If you prefer draft beer, ask for a *birra alla spina*.

2
Ancient and Medieval Rome

As the birthplace of Rome, the old part of the city is imbued with Classical history. Arches, columns, pavements or even walls remain from Republican and Imperial Rome, many incorporated into later buildings, others openly stolen and used for building materials, or decoration, elsewhere. And, surprisingly, contemporary excavations for modern civic projects sometimes still reveal the presence of buildings hitherto unknown to us.

For over 1000 years, this part of town was the heart of the Roman Empire. Rome celebrated its first millennium in AD247 when most other areas of Europe were fending off feuding tribes and struggling for survival. From this Classical era, the various **Fora** remain, broken buildings hinting at the glorious architecture that once graced this civic centre and meeting place. The **Colosseum**, Vespasian's largest architectural legacy and a focal point in Rome, continues to pack in the crowds, though today they are tourists wielding cameras rather than gladiators with swords. Nero's oversized residence, the **Domus Aurea** – his so-called Golden House – has finally been renovated, and revealed to the public after decades of closure, while the leafy **Palatine Hill**, former home to the more humble **Emperor Augustus** and his wife Livia, provides a little elysian pleasure in the heart of the city.

On a foundation of Classical Roman ruins, Medieval Rome built its monuments. The fascinating church of **San Clemente** and the basilica of **San Giovanni in Laterano** document the rise of Christianity – and its continuing endurance – in this Holy City.

DON'T MISS

*** **The Forum:** by day and by night, the view from behind Piazza Campidoglio is superb.
*** **The Colosseum:** especially breathtaking when viewed by full moon.
** **Terme di Caracalla:** the baths of Caracalla.
* **Palatine Hill:** a good spot for a picnic!
* **San Clemente:** see the beautiful mosaics and the ancient foundations.
* **San Giovanni in Laterano:** one of Rome's four basilicas.

◄ *Opposite: The fragrant flower stalls in the Piazza Vittorio market.*

▶ *Right: The three remaining columns of the temple of Castor and Pollux, Roman Forum.*

THE VITTORIANO

Undoubtedly the largest monument in Rome, if not its most subtle, this vast white extravaganza was built between 1885 and 1911 to celebrate **Vittorio Emanuele II**, the first king of a united Italy. Italy's Tomb of the Unknown Soldier was added after WWI and there are also a couple of military museums inside. It climbs up the side of the **Capitoline Hill**, formerly the sacred and administrative heart of ancient Rome. You can climb to the top for spectacular views. For the **Piazza Venezia**, see page 52; for the **Campidoglio**, see page 54.

THE FORA

Originally marshland between Rome's seven hills, this lowland zone became the meeting and trading point between the various groups that inhabited the surrounding hills during the 1st millennium BC. The **Fora** – actually a series of successive Fora built by the first rulers, then emperors Caesar, Augustus, Trajan and Nerva – are so ruined and intermixed that it is hard to get a clear grasp of their layout. They are best seen, at first, from the **Capitoline Hill** (*see* page 54).

Today's broad avenue, **Via dei Fori Imperiali** that runs from Piazza Venezia to the Colosseum, divides the Fora. The magnificent **Roman Forum** (the most important of the sites) lies to the south and the **Fori Imperiali** lie to its north. The Fora are open daily and an admission fee is payable.

Il Foro Romano (Roman Forum) ***

The **Sacra Via**, which runs through the centre of this ancient forum, served as a processional route taken by victorious generals. It leads from the 4th-century **Arch of Constantine** via the imposing **Arch of Titus**, built in AD81 by Domitian in memory of his brother, into the heart of the Roman Forum.

On the right are the remains of the large **Temple of Venus and Rome**, built in AD135 by Hadrian who may also have designed it. The elegant, slim **Temple of Antoninus and Faustina** was erected in AD141 by Antoninus Pius in memory of his wife, Faustina, and also shelters an 11th-century church, San Lorenzo.

Reflect for a moment at the **Temple of Caesar**, on the spot where Caesar was cremated and Mark Anthony made his funerary oration. Sometimes, there are small offerings of flowers to the far-from-forgotten ruler. The circular **Temple of Vesta**, rebuilt in AD191, was where the sacred flame – the synonym for the continuation of the Roman state – was kept. Nearby, the three remaining

▲ *Above: Home to Rome's sacred flame, the Temple of Vesta now has but three columns.*

Roman Forum

Via dei Fori Imperiali
Largo Romolo e Remo
Fori Imperiali
Via S. Vecchia
Basilica of Constantine
Piazza di San Francesca Romana
Temple of Venus and Rome
Colosseum
Piazza del Colosseo
Temple of Saturn
Basilica Aemilia
Temple of Antoninus and Faustina
Curia
Arch of Septimius Severus
Temple of Caesar
Via Sacra
Foro Romano
Arch of Titus
Arch of Constantine
Via Sacra
Palazzo Senatorio
Temple of the Castors
Temple of Vesta
Basilica Giulia
Temple of Vespasian and Titus
Via S. Teodoro
Santa Maria Antiqua
0   100 m
0   100 yd

columns from the **Temple of the Dioscuri**, part of the cult of Castor and Pollux, are all that are left of the original 484BC temple.

Judging by the seven remaining columns, the **Temple of Saturn**, consecrated in 498BC but rebuilt in 42BC, must have been huge, towering over the beautiful **Arch of Septimius Severus**, built in AD203 and dedicated to the former emperor by his son, Caracalla. Look out for the **Curia**, where the Roman Senate used to meet and the remaining Corinthian columns of the **Temple of Vespasian and Titus**.

Fori Imperiali (Imperial Fora) *

This complex of Fora (not open to the public, although you can see perfectly well from the road above) was built by five successive emperors and filled with monuments and libraries. This was also where most political, religious and commercial functions were held. Still distinguishable are the white marble columns of the **Temple of Mars Ultor**, erected in 42BC, and the semi-circular porticoes, whose niches were once embellished with statues. The northern portico ended in the **Hall of the Colossus**, which once housed several impressive works of art.

Trajan's Rome **

Beside the Vittoriano, the beautiful **Colonna di Traiano**, or Trajan's Column, is one of the finest examples of Roman bas-relief remaining today. Commissioned by Hadrian and dedicated to Trajan in commemoration of the successful 2nd-century military campaigns against the Dacians (modern-day Romania), it is a masterpiece of carving. A spiral frieze winds its way up the column, showing various phases of the campaign, bas-reliefs that were once, though not now, easily readable from the

surrounding monuments. The massive redbrick building next door is the recently renovated **Trajan's Forum** and **Market** (open daily, a fee is payable), built by Trajan at the beginning of the 2nd century. Truly remarkable, these 150 shops and offices, laid out on various floors in an arc surrounding the forum, were the forerunners of today's massive shopping malls, and provide a vivid image of the day-to-day life of ancient Rome.

THE COLOSSEUM AND BEYOND

Fabulous archaeological sites, parks and pleasant residential roads characterize the area around the Colosseum. Within walking distance of the famous amphitheatre are the **Domus Aurea**, **San Clemente**, the **Palatine Hill** and **Piazza Venezia** (see page 52).

The Colosseum ★★★

Seventy-six numbered entrances and four VIP entrances lead into this huge elliptical amphitheatre commissioned by the greatest Flavian emperor, **Vespasian**. It came to be known as the Colosseum, it is believed, because of the colossal bronze statue of **Nero** that once stood nearby.

EMPERORS OF ROME

In 44BC, the Roman general **Julius Caesar** declared himself Emperor, but was assassinated a month later. Seventeen years of fighting ensued until his adopted son, **Octavian**, was proclaimed Emperor Augustus in 27BC, the first of a long line of nearly 80 emperors before the fall of Rome in AD476. Some of the most memorable include:
27BC–AD14 – Augustus
AD14–37 – Tiberius
AD37–41 – Caligula
AD41–54 – Claudius
AD54–68 – Nero
AD69–79 – Vespasian
AD98–117 – Trajan
AD117–138 – Hadrian
AD161–180 – Marcus Aurelius
AD193–211 – Septimius Severus
AD211–217 – Caracalla
AD285–305 – Diocletian
AD306–337 – Constantine the Great

◀◀ *Opposite: The curving façade of Trajan's market.*
◀ *Left: Much damaged by traffic pollution, the rear of the Colosseum rises to its original four storeys.*

**MERCATO DI PIAZZA
VITTORIO EMANUELE II**

Ginger, mangoes, soya, dried fish and pungent chillies do not readily spring to mind when you think of Italian markets, but the large street market around picturesque **Piazza V. Emanuele** is the focal point for **African** and **Asian** ingredients. Fresh or dried. Italian fruit and vegetables also feature. Get there early for the best buys – and watch your bags in the crowds. Open 07:00–14:00, Monday to Saturday.

Capable of holding between 50 and 85,000 spectators – and of emptying in less than 10 minutes – the building witnessed some of the bloodiest combats in the history of the Empire (*see* panel on page 34).

Gladiatorial combats continued until AD407, and fights with wild beasts until AD422 when Christianity, and its values, began to take hold on a declining Rome. These marathon spectacles, staged by the Emperor and his elite, were open to all, free of charge, and – according to their rank – individuals made their way to the appropriate section reserved for people of their own standing; the elite occupying the lower tiers; the bottom of the social ladder, and women, taking the top sections of the amphitheatre.

Below the arena, a labyrinth of corridors and rooms housed machinery, men and beasts. Over this a wooden floor was laid, topped with sand (to prevent combatants from slipping and to absorb the blood). The entire area was covered by a vellum roof, which was secured to posts around the circumference and remains of these still exist. Along the ground level, and under the seating, was the *vomitorium* where ablutions took place.

Today, it is possible to visit most parts of the Colosseum and find a quiet stop from where to contemplate its 1900 years of history. And, to add a little more suspense, guided evening tours are offered twice weekly during summer months. Open daily.

▶ *Opposite: San Clemente, near the Colosseum, rises over the remains of an earlier temple venerating Mithras, the Persian god of light.*
▼ *Below: Coronation of the Virgin, by Raphael.*

Arch of Constantine *

Built as a triumphal monument in AD315, this arch was erected to commemorate the Emperor's victory at the **Battle of the Milvian Bridge**. It does, however, sadly reflect the decline of the Empire for Constantine's architects pilfered earlier works to create this arch. Only the bottom section was carved for the Emperor – and what poor work it is in comparison with the beautifully hewn panels removed from work probably commissioned by the great Trajan.

Domus Aurea (Golden House) *

Northeast of the Colosseum lies the Domus Aurea, the **Golden House**, a vast palace built by the megalomaniac, Nero. Though in concept very exciting, the fact is that despite recent renovation and its historic opening to the public, there is nothing golden about it today. Centre of Nero's universe, his house radiates out from an octagonal dining room. Some of the walls and ceilings are still painted with exquisite frescoes (once including gold details), and the house had baths, pools and scores of reception rooms. On

Nero's death, the gardens and lakes were drained, and as Trajan built over the Domus Aurea, its existence was largely forgotten. In Renaissance times, such great artists as **Raphael** lowered themselves into the ruins and marvelled at the stucco-work and paintings; some of these artists went so far as to leave graffiti attesting to their visit. Closed on Tuesdays.

San Clemente *

Not far from the Colosseum, and near the Domus Aurea, is the church of San Clemente, Via di San Giovanni in Laterano. It is a quirky church with some fine floor mosaics, but the real attraction here is to descend into the bowels of the building to discover the remains of the previous churches on which the present building was erected. Medieval mosaics (in rather poor condition) decorate walls of the former church while in the dark, dank corridors below there are vestiges of a temple consecrated to the cult of **Mithras**, the Persian god of light, who was a favoured god among early Romans. And, as you shiver through these daunting areas, you will hear – and see – vestiges of ancient drains carrying water.

WATER, WATER EVERYWHERE ...

And there is more than a drop to drink. It's thirst-quenching, tastes good and, best of all, it's free. The Ancient Romans took water seriously – you have only to look at the remains of the vast *terme* (baths) to realize this. They brought fresh water to Rome via a series of purpose-built **aqueducts**, parts of which are still extant in and around the city. **Conduits** were laid to a series of elaborate **fountains**, bringing fresh drinking water to the citizen in the street. Fountains became more decorative and less functional during the Baroque period but visitors will find plenty of street fountains with potable, pleasantly cool water throughout town.

▲ *Above: The remains of Caracalla's huge baths illustrate the importance these fitness centres played in ancient times.*

Il Palatino (Palatine Hill) *

A peaceful area of lush greenery, the renowned Palatine Hill combines history and relaxation. It was here, on one of the seven original hills of Rome, that **Romulus and Remus** were – according to legend – raised by the she-wolf. Traces of Iron-Age settlements have been found here dating back to 700– 800BC.

In Republican and early Imperial Roman days, the Palatine Hill was a smart address: **Augustus** and his wife, **Livia**, lived here, so too did **Cicero**, **Tiberius** and **Caligula**. Accessible from the **Roman Forum**, this area combines the ruins of both public and private imperial buildings interspersed with shady trees and grassy banks.

Built in two sections, the **Domus Augustana** (which was named not after the Emperor, but for the 'august' leaders) was the private residence of Domitian (AD81–96) and it remained home to his successors over the following 300 years. The **Domus Flavia** was built as an official palace, and the nearby, rather humble **Domus Livia** was where Augustus lived with his wife, Livia.

Lastly, make time to linger in the **Farnese Gardens**. These botanical gardens were created by Cardinal Alessandro Farnese on the ground where Tiberius' palace once stood.

FURTHER AFIELD

Architectural highlights further afield include the magnificent ruins of the **Baths of Caracalla** on the road out towards **EUR** (Mussolini's purpose-built city started in 1938). About a kilometre northeast of the Baths, stands the **Basilica of San Giovanni in Laterano**, one of the four large basilicas that enjoy a special reputation in Rome.

Terme di Caracalla (Baths of Caracalla) **

Better known as the site of historic concerts, this large complex was started by Emperor Caracalla in AD212, but was finished only after his death. It was conceived to be what we would think of today as a huge leisure drome – a fitness centre with gardens, libraries and recreational areas capable of housing 1600 people – for the Romans believed that the body and the mind should be kept in trim.

Remains of the *caldarium* (hot baths) can be seen on the exterior, the huge arches protecting the *tepidarium* (warm baths) and *frigidarium* (cold baths), and parts of the gymnasia, are all distinguishable. Some of the finest sculptures found here are now part of the Farnese Collection in the Archaeological Museum in Naples. Open daily.

Basilica di San Giovanni in Laterano *

The **Piazza di San Giovanni in Laterano** is a large, imposing square, set out in the 16th century around an Egyptian obelisk and lined with stately buildings. On its eastern side lies the Basilica of San Giovanni in Laterano, a huge building comprising a church as well as adjoining palaces and cloisters. It dates back to the 4th century when land was seized by **Constantine** and used to construct the first Christian basilica. Subsequently, it was the centre of **Roman Christianity** and the popes resided in the **Lateran Palace** until their flight to Avignon. On their return, they stayed near St Peter's.

In Borromini's breathtaking interior, look for reconstructed mosaics in the apse, the Gothic *baldacchino*, the Medieval cloisters with their delightful mosaic columns and the baptistery. The impressive façade, topped with sculptures of Christ and the apostles, was created in 1735 by **Alessandro Galilei**.

SANTA CROCE IN GERUSALEMME

The Church of Santa Croce, in the piazza of the same name just a five-minute bus ride from **San Giovanni**, holds one of Christendom's most prized relics: a fragment of the **True Cross**, the **Santa Croce**. You can easily decipher the remains of the carved inscription and, nearby, a full facsimile of Pontius Pilate's inscription – Jesus of Nazareth King of the Jews – in Greek, Latin and Hebrew. The church was built, it is said, by Constantine's mother, **St Helena**, in the grounds of her palace around AD320. In the attractive crypt there is a modified Roman sculpture of **Juno** to which a cross has been added, the head and arms changed to represent St Helena.

▼ *Below: An 18th-century Christ and the apostles crown the façade of San Giovanni in Laterano.*

3. Il Quirinale, Via Veneto and Stazione di Termini

One of the highest points in Rome, *Il Quirinale* (or **Quirinal Hill**, one of Rome's seven hills) rose to fashion in the 16th century when **Pope Gregory XIII** decided he required a healthier environment than the area around St Peter's for weathering the hot summer months, and so built a new palace. The area continued to grow in popularity and a number of wealthy Roman families constructed palaces there. Today it is the official residence of the president of the Republic, and many government, insurance and bank buildings have been erected in the vicinity. It is an area largely built in the 18th and 19th centuries – the streets are wide and straight, and lined with large dignified buildings.

Also of the 19th century, **Via Veneto** is less imposing, a street for leisure and pleasure, for strolling and dining. Once the favourite haunt of the *glitterati*, it is now filled with more tourists than locals.

To the east, across the busy **Via Nazionale** and **Via Cavour** – both bustling commercial arteries – the neighbourhood loses some of its chic. The Roma Stazione Termini, or **Termini**, is the city's main and recently modernized railway station. Incongruously located opposite are the Classical remains of the *Terme di Diocleziano*, the huge Baths of Diocletian, but to the south, a different atmosphere prevails as African and Asian immigrants have moved into the area, bringing spice and rice to the neighbourhood. In its midst, **Santa Maria Maggiore**, one of the city's great basilicas, stands proud as the reminder of another era and another culture.

Don't Miss

*** Palazzo Massimo:** houses part of the Museo Nazionale Romano, with its ancient sculpture and beautiful mosaics.
** Piazza Quirinale: elegant seat of Italy's government.
** Palazzo Barberini: see the gallery and beautifully decorated rooms.
** San Carlo alle Quattro Fontane: pure baroque splendour.
** Via Veneto: take a nostalgic stroll and enjoy a drink.
*** Fontana di Trevi:** toss a coin for luck!

◀ *Opposite: A glimpse of the Baroque church, Santi Domenico e Sisto.*

PALAZZO COLONNA AND BEYOND

A pleasant neighbourhood in which tourists rarely linger, the lower slopes of the **Quirinal Hill** offer visitors several points of interest, including Rome's most romantic fountain, the Trevi.

Fontana di Trevi (Trevi Fountain) *

To ensure that you will return to Rome, so they say, toss a coin over your opposite shoulder and into the fountain. Toss two to meet a Roman, toss three for marriage. It's such enduring folklore – and the wonderful Baroque sculpture – that bring the crowds to **Trevi Fountain**. The sound of tumbling water fills the air, couples pose for photographs and souvenir salesmen fare well. Dominating the piazza of the same name, **Neptune**, god of the sea, bursts from an elaborate Baroque façade, while two tritons tussle with sea creatures. It was built for Pope Clement XII by Nicolo Salvi in 1762 at the point where the Acqua Vergine, ancient Rome's main acqueduct, ended.

▼ *Below: Completed in 1762, the Fontana di Trevi is one of the capital's most elaborate fountains.*

While walking back down **Via Muratte**, look at the 20th-century building (an office and apartment block) on the left, where every surface of its courtyard is decorated with paintings and designs.

Palazzo Colonna *

The main reason for visiting the Palazzo is to view the **Galleria Colonna** (Saturday mornings only), a fine collection of 17th- and 18th-century Roman paintings, in impressive Baroque surrounds. Unfortunately the canvases are mostly unlabelled, therefore a guide is indispensable. Among the most notable works are those by Domenico and Jacopo Tintoretto, Dughet, Guercino, Bronzino, Carracci and del Sarto.

Villa Aldobrandini *

Though this 16th-century villa is closed to visitors, its garden is open (the entrance is on via Mazzarino 1) and provides a welcome respite in an area that has few public squares or tree-filled streets. Stairs lead past 2nd-century ruins to a small formal garden decorated with plenty of headless Roman sculptures. From Villa Aldobrandini, it's just a short walk to visit the church of **Santi Domenico e Sisto**, a very slim Baroque church with an impressive façade, rising above a rather grandiose flight of stairs.

▲ Above: Quiet corners around the Fontana di Trevi are filled with cafés, ideal for a quick reviver.

Sant'Agata dei Goti (St Agatha of the Goths) *

Behind a plain entrance on **Via Panisperna** (or Mazzarino 16) lies the small and tranquil church of **St Agatha of the Goths**, which dates back to the latter half of the 5th century. While Agatha's agonies are very aptly outlined in the series of paintings decorating the upper storey of the church, the ancient columns and decorative capitals are almost overlooked. Many visitors are more taken with the small courtyard outside, which is filled with plants and trees.

The area around Sant'Agata is one of Rome's prime business districts. The imposing **Banca d'Italia**, the country's central bank, takes up an entire block on **Via Nazionale**. Built at the end of the 19th century it, too, has been recently renovated. Further north along Via Nazionale lies the grandiose **Palazzo delle Esposizioni**. This building has also been renovated and it now accommodates a changing cycle of contemporary exhibitions and shows. Note the tiny church, a few steps away. Below the level of the road, **San Vitale** has been restored and remodelled many times since its consecration in AD416. The exterior is, to many, more interesting than the interior.

CATCH THE BUS!

8 – Modern tram linking Monteverde and Trastevere with Largo di Torre Argentina.
44 – From Piazza Venezia to Trastevere.
64 – From Termini to St Peter's, via Piazza Venezia.
116 – Electric mini-bus from Via Giulia, via the Pantheon to Piazza Barberini and Via Veneto.
117 – Electric mini-bus from Piazza del Popolo to Via del Corso, Piazza Venezia and San Giovanni in Laterano.
119 – Electric mini-bus from Piazza del Popolo, Via del Corso, Piazza Venezia, Piazza Barberini, Piazza di Spagna to Piazza del Popolo.
492 – Stazione Tiburtina, Termini, Piazza Venezia to Piazza Risorgimento.
760 – From Piazza Venezia to the Baths of Caracalla and beyond.

▶ *Opposite: The vivid colours of the Quirinal Palace distinguish the official residence of Italy's state president.*

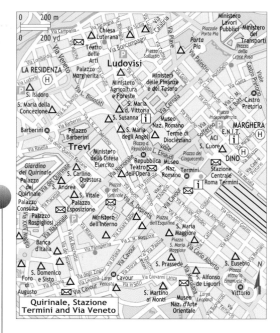

Quirinale, Stazione Termini and Via Veneto

Born in Naples, Bernini's father was a noted Tuscan sculptor who moved to work in Rome when Bernini was a child. At the age of just 17, the young Bernini was already working for papal cardinals, and created a number of exquisite sculptures for **Cardinal Scipione Borghese** including the *Rape of Proserpina, David*, and *Apollo and Daphne* (all in the **Museo Borghese**). Although he was much influenced by **Michelangelo** and antiquities, he also admired his contemporaries, especially **Annibale Carracci** and **Guido Reni**. A passionate, sometimes violent man, and also a devout **Christian**, Bernini freed his sculptures from their blocks and encouraged spectators to walk around them, to become part of their space. This concept underlined his architecture too, and ensured he became Baroque's greatest exponent. One has only to look at his works at **St Peter's** or the **Cornaro Chapel** to appreciate this.

AROUND IL QUIRINALE

One of Rome's smartest areas, the Quirinal Hill is home to the Italian leader and is also a venue for meetings with politicians and world leaders. Only a few buses serve *Il Quirinale*, so it is best to explore on foot.

Palazzo del Quirinale **

Occupying a large square at the top of the Quirinal Hill, dominated by the statue and fountain, and guarded not only by the **Carabinieri** but by the enormously tall presidential guards, lies the Palazzo del Quirinale. The list of architects concerned at some stage of its construction notes all the most active in Baroque Rome. It includes designs by Flaminio Ponzio, Domenico Fontana, Carlo Maderno, Gianlorenzo Bernini and Fernando Fuga.

Within the Palazzo, the **Scuderie del Quirinale** holds fine-art exhibitions between September and June. The palace itself dominates the piazza, enclosing magnificent formal gardens and affording the privileged sweeping views across Rome. This stately building, once the summer residence of 16th-century popes, became, in the late 19th century, the residence of the kings of Italy. Since reverting to a Republic, the palace has now assumed the role of official residence and office of the president.

Be sure to give the central statue a moment of contemplation, for it is a very attractive Roman copy of a Greek statue depicting **Castor and Pollux**, which dated from the 5th century BC. Towering over the powerful horses and their masters is an obelisk that was brought from Augustus' tomb.

Sant'Andrea al Quirinale *

Near the small Quirinale gardens is Sant'Andrea al Quirinale (via del Quirinale 29), a plain, yellow façade that belies the richness of the church's lavish interior. With an unusual elliptical-shaped floor plan (the site was broader than it was deep) and lovely pale pink marble, this Bernini-designed church is a gem. Started in 1658 for the Jesuits, the church was finished just 12 years later. **Bernini** conceived it as a whole and was instrumental in the commissioning of sculpture and paintings. The altarpiece, a **Crucifixion of Saint Andrew** by Il Borgognone, depicts the saint who, in turn, looks out of the painting and up at a sculpted version of himself, ascending into heaven.

San Carlino alle Quattro Fontane **

Once again, **Borromini**, Bernini's great rival, has left a fabulous legacy just steps away from a Bernini site. The church of San Carlino Quattro Fontane – erected where two thoroughfares meet and a fountain was created on each corner – is one of the artist's greatest works. The church (entrance at via del Quirinale 23) and cloister, commissioned by the Spanish Trinitarians in 1634, was finished in 1667. Like the

BERNINI'S ROME

Indulge yourself with some of the master's best works:
• **Santa Maria della Vittoria**: *The Ecstasy of St Teresa.*
• **San Francesco a Ripa**: *The Ecstasy of Beata Ludovica Albertona.*
• The church of **Sant'Andrea al Quirinale**.
• **Santa Maria del Popolo**: individual sculptures.
• **Palazzo Montecitorio**: parliament
• The fountain in **Piazza di Spagna**.
• The **Fontana dei Quattro Fiumi** in Piazza Navona.
• The **Fontana del Tritone** in Piazza Barberini.
• Sculpture of an elephant and an ancient obelisk in **Piazza Santa Maria sopra Minerva**.
• The sculpted angels on **Ponte Sant'Angelo**.
• The *baldacchino* and the tomb of **Alexander VII** in St Peter's.
• The sculpture in **Museo Borghese**.

former church, space was cramped but with a series of concave and convex walls, an oval dome and intricate, light stucco, the interior seems far larger than on plan. A crypt below the church remains empty. It is thought that the architect wished to be buried there.

VIA VENETO

Once *the* place to be seen, 19th-century Via Veneto enjoyed a glorious social life during Federico Fellini's heyday and the golden days of Italian cinema. The grandiose hotels along its rising curve hosted divas and directors, while film fans lingered along the avenue in the hopes of being transported, for a moment, by the magic of their movie stars. Today, the russet leaves of its tall plane trees rustle in the gutter and the elegant hotels have an air of another, more luxurious era. It is altogether a more sober street – even its signature pavement cafés have been glassed in, caging the café and apéritif society. Elderly matrons, arm in arm with their escorts, walk dogs and reminisce. But Via Veneto seems to be coming into vogue once again, enjoying a renewed vigor with a younger crowd of patrons.

Off Piazza Barberini, the crypt of the **Capuchin Church of the Immaculate** contains the bones of some 4300 monks, delicately arranged in charmingly rococo patterns. It sounds – and is – bizarre, but is surprisingly uncreepy.

VICE ON VIA VENETO

There are increasing tales concerning less than scrupulous, attractive, young people who are befriending single foreigners strolling the Via Veneto area. They invite them for a drink in one of those cosy, darkened bars before relieving them of their valuables. If you accept an invitation, never leave your valuables unattended, and always sit in a well-lit part of the establishment.

Piazza Barberini and Palazzo Barberini **

Not Rome's most attractive square, despite Bernini's superb **Fontana del Tritone**, this open space needs some trees to soften the unappealing architecture. However, in the days of the **Barberini** family, it was just a stone's throw from the Palazzo Barberini, built for **Maffei Barberini** (Pope Urban VIII) by architects Maderno, Bernini and

Borromini. It's a somewhat fading palace that now houses one of the city's prime museums, part of the **Galleria Nazionale d'Arte Antica** (entrance on via delle Quattro Fontane 13). Massive, though attractive in its solidity, the palace today sits amid a neighbourhood of less attractive commercial buildings. The most impressive feature is one of Pietro da Cortona's

works, the *Triumph of Divine Providence*, a marvellous, illusionistic ceiling fresco in the **Gran Salone**.

▲ Above: A trompe l'œil ceiling fresco crowns one of the staterooms in the Palazzo Barberini.
◄ Opposite: The ageing Palazzo Barberini houses a fine picture gallery.

Among the highlights of the Galleria are works by Tintoretto, El Greco, Titian, Lorenzo Lotto, Bronzino, Beccafumi, Guido Reni, Crespi, Nicolas Poussin and a painting of a woman considered Raphael's mistress, the so-called 'Fornarina'. There is also a fine portrait of England's Henry VIII, attributed to Holbein. Also open on the top floor are the rooms that were inhabited until the middle of the 20th century by the last of the Barberini family. The walls are skillfully painted in a variety of beautiful and fragile designs. Closed on Mondays.

Santa Susanna and Santa Maria della Vittoria *

Almost side by side, separated only by Largo Santa Susanna, are two impressive Baroque churches with earlier origins. **Santa Susanna** is a masterpiece by Carlo Maderno where **Baldassarre Croce's** fabulous, ornate frescoes (painted, in 1595, to imitate tapestries) deserve a visit. This Catholic church is also used by the American community in Rome and has services in English daily.

The main reason for visiting Santa Maria della Vittoria is usually to see Bernini's **Cornaro Chapel** with a riveting sculpture of Santa Teresa, a saint who, having been stabbed by an angel holding an arrow, is in the throes of ecstasy as she is about to be martyred. Observing the

PIETRO DA CORTONA (1596–1669)

Born **Pietro Berrettini** in Cortona, this artist reached the same heights in painting as Bernini did in sculpture. The **Barberini** family soon became his patrons and he was invited to paint the soaring ceiling frescoes *Allegory of Divine Providence* and *Barberini Power* in the **Palazzo Barberini**, probably his most breathtaking work. Cortona has flawlessly mastered the art of perspective, extending his theme right into the corners and creating a superb illusionistic work that defies the boundaries of the salon.

scene are sculptures of various members of the Cornaro family, patrons of the chapel.

STAZIONE TERMINI AREA

East of Via Veneto, Rome's main station has been renovated to include some excellent shops, a gallery and various cafés. There are several sights worth seeing in the area near the station. Among these are the **Terme di Diocleziano**, the **Museo Nazionale Romano** (in the Palazzo Massimo) and the huge basilica of **Santa Maria Maggiore**.

Terme di Diocleziano (Baths of Diocletian) *

Located in today's **Piazza del Cinquecento**, these were the largest baths in Rome and could accommodate over 3000 people. Only parts survive for modern Rome has encroached on their historic foundations. Certain areas of the Baths, built in AD298–306 by Diocletian and Maximian, remain open to the visitor, while others are incorporated into buildings such as the **Carthusian Convent** and church of **Santa Maria degli Angeli**. Michelangelo was responsible for the design of this building in the 1550s and, had he finished it himself, it would undoubtedly have become one of Rome's most beautiful churches. The Michelangelo cloister has now been renovated as part of an excellent new museum, filled with Roman statuary and epigraphy, which is part of the National Museum collection. Closed on Mondays.

Palazzo Massimo ***

In 1998, many of the priceless exhibits from the **Museo Nazionale Romano** were moved to the beautifully renovated Palazzo Massimo, diagonally across Piazza del Cinquecento; others remain in the **Diocletian Baths** while a further collection is housed in the **Palazzo Altemps**.

▲ *Above: The magnificent Palazzo Massimo proves to be one of the city's most impressive museums.*
▶ *Opposite: A bust of the Emperor Vespasian, who ruled from ad69–79, in the Palazzo Massimo.*

GREAT ROMAN CITIZENS

- **Cicero** (lawyer and philosopher) 106–43BC
- **Hadrian** (a Spaniard; emperor and architect) AD76–138
- **Horace** (poet) 65–8BC
- **Livy** (writer and dramatist) 59BC–AD17
- **Ovid** (poet) 43BC–AD17/18
- **Pliny the Elder** (Roman naturalist) AD23–75
- **Pliny the Younger** (nephew of Pliny the Elder: writer) AD62–114
- **Virgil** (poet) 70–19BC

This collection of Roman sculpture, wall painting, mosaics, early jewellery and coins is one of the most exciting and accessible in the city and constitutes one of Italy's most important collections.

Pride of the museum is the extraordinarily beautiful reconstructed room from **Livia's House**, a dining room painted to recreate the countryside, complete with birds, plants and flowers. On the same floor is the interior of an ancient Roman villa found in the grounds of **Villa Farnesina**. The pitch-black room is decorated with sublime small, coloured paintings of mythological scenes and landscapes linked by painted festoons. Nearby is the collection of magnificent mosaics, some so delicate they seem more like paintings; these once formed the floors of patrician homes. Book ahead on timed tickets to see the frescoes. A fine series of low-relief sculptures from the 2nd century AD depict the costumes of Roman *cives* in different parts of the Empire. Also on the ground floor are scores of Greek, and copies of Greek, sculptural masterpieces. Many of the sculptures found at Hadrian's Villa in Tivoli (*see* page 112) are now housed here. Closed on Mondays.

FACE TO FACE WITH THE FAMOUS

The collection of ancient busts in **Palazzo Massimo** is fascinating. Beautifully displayed, you can take stock of **Caligula**, Nero's wife, **Poppea**, **Vespasian**, **Hadrian**, **Marcus Aurelius**, **Septimius Severus** or **Caracalla** and, with the subtle use of spot lights, they are uncannily real. It is a good opportunity to get to grips with the complex chronology of the Roman emperors and their immediate families.

Santa Maria Maggiore *

Not in the most attractive part of Rome, Santa Maria Maggiore (in the square of the same name) nevertheless attracts the crowds as this large basilica is a homogenous blend of architectural elements tracing its 1500 years of history. Both the west façade (with sweeping stairs) and the east façade (with Baroque columns and arches) are arresting, but the Medieval mosaics hold the most interest. Constructed in 1295, the mosaic *Coronation of the Virgin* in the church's apse is a marvel. So too is the tomb of **Cardinal Rodriguez**, which dates from the same era. The Cardinal is portrayed smiling as he prays. The side chapels, one built for Pope Paul V Borghese and the other for Pope Sixtus V, are richly decorated Baroque and Renaissance works.

4. Il Campidoglio, Jewish Rome and Campo de' Fiori

The smallest of the seven hills of Rome, **Il Campidoglio**, or the Capitoline Hill, occupied as long ago as the Bronze Age, still enjoys a central position in today's city. The **Forum** was the heart of Ancient Rome, yet today it is surrounded by Renaissance, Baroque and Risorgimento buildings marking first the kingdom and then the modern Republic of Italy. Architect Michelangelo created a harmonious order in the **Piazza del Campidoglio** where the **Capitoline Museums**, boasting one of the world's finest collections of art, are housed in the buildings on either side.

Looking westward from the Capitoline, and beyond the ruins of **Marcellus' Theatre**, the dome of the **Synagogue** is just distinguishable, marking the Jewish part of Rome, known as the **Ghetto**. Vestiges of this once off-limits area still remain and the 350 years during which Jews suffered under Christians are not forgotten. However, this part of town is becoming increasingly fashionable; there are plenty of *trattorie* and restaurants and Jewish cuisine is enjoying a revival.

Further afield, beyond the site of Julius Caesar's murder, **Area Sacra** and the **Largo di Torre Argentina**, lies the **Campo de' Fiori**, formerly a meadow of flowers, and now a popular square with a colourful morning market. In the neighbourhood are some of Rome's finest Renaissance palaces, such as the solid **Palazzo Farnese** and brilliant white **Palazzo della Cancelleria**, and within some of these, museums housing exhibits from over 2500 years of Western civilization.

DON'T MISS

*** Piazza Campidoglio: Michelangelo's beautiful symmetrical creation.
*** Capitoline Museums: ancient Greek and Roman sculptural masterpieces.
** Campo de' Fiori: visit the morning market.
** Palazzo Spada: be sure to see Borromini's impressive trompe l'œil corridor.
** Santa Maria Cosmedin: a beautiful ancient church.
** Church of the Gesù: admire the ornate interior.
* Ghetto: stroll through the Jewish section of Rome.

◄ *Opposite: The ancient amphorae of Testaccio in a modern sculpture.*

PIAZZA VENEZIA

The meeting point for many travellers, Piazza Venezia lies in the heart of Rome. On one side is **Palazzo Venezia**, on the opposite is a complementary Renaissance palace with Venetian emblems, while the whole square is dominated by the enormous, snowy white **Monumento a Vittorio Emanuele II**, also known as **Il Vittoriano** (see page 32). This 1911 monument, which has been variously described as a wedding cake, a typewriter and a set of dentures, was erected in honour of the king who unified Italy.

SPQR

Everywhere in Rome, these initials appear: on manhole covers, civil buildings, public transport or in ancient inscriptions. They stand for **Senatus Populusque Romanus** – the Senate and People of Rome – and were used much in the same way as a city council might put its stamp on civic works today. The difference is, these initials were first used nearly 2000 years ago and continue to be used today.

Palazzo Venezia *

The rust-coloured Palazzo Venezia was built in 1455 for the Venetian Cardinal Pietro Baro (later Pope Paul II) and has, at various times, served as a papal residence. During the 19th century, it was the residence for the Austrian ambassador to the Vatican. It was also used by Mussolini who delivered some of his speeches from the prominent balcony facing the square. Today, its palm-filled courtyard has lost its harmony to the scrum of cars and motorbikes that treat it as a parking lot.

Palazzo Venezia houses a fine museum, the **Museo del Palazzo Venezia** (the entrance is at via del Plebiscito 118), which is too often overlooked by tourists. Included in its exhibits are some rare ivories from the 8th century, a good collection of early and mid-Renaissance paintings, ceramics from the best porcelain factories

Campidoglio and Jewish Rome

in Europe, scores of small bronzes, and a collection of terracotta models (in preparation for sculpture and bronzes) from such illustrious masters as Bernini. The museum is closed on Mondays.

Santissimo Nome di Gesù (Church of the Gesù) ★★

Along the busy east–west axis, Corso Vittorio Emanuele II, and at **Piazza Gesù**, lies the first Jesuit church to be built in Rome, the Gesù. An elaborate masterpiece created between 1568 and 1584 by architects **Giacomo della Porta** and **Vignola** (responsible for the highly decorative interior), the Gesù was the prototype of an architectural largesse which was to characterize subsequent Jesuit buildings.

On first entering the church, its interior can be quite overwhelming. Every available surface is elaborately decorated: columns, pilasters, walls, ceiling and the cupola. The ceiling above the nave is a vigorous trompe l'œil, the *Triumph of the Name of Jesus* painted by Il Baciccia, where statues and soaring painted figures interact. It takes the task of perspective to its utmost extremes and succeeds beautifully.

▲ *Above: The plain exterior of Santa Maria in Aracoeli belies its lovely interior.*
◄ *Opposite: Colourful, elegant and graced by Venetian-style palaces, Piazza Venezia lies at the heart of Rome.*

Santa Maria in Aracoeli ★

Behind **Il Vittoriano**, past the bus terminus and towards the summit of the Capitoline Hill, lies the church of Santa Maria in Aracoeli. The long, forbidding flight of 123 stairs up to its drab brick façade (there is also an entrance from the east side of the Campidoglio) belies the beauty of this church's interior.

First built in the 7th century, it is today predominantly Medieval and early Renaissance in style. The columns defining the nave were taken from Roman sites, while chandeliers light up the gilt, geometric ceiling, giving the interior an unparalleled elegance. An icon of the **Holy Child**, in a side chapel, is reputed to have miraculous powers and it attracts thousands of wishful worshippers.

LATIN VESTIGES IN MODERN ENGLISH

Who said Latin was dead? It is surprising just how many Latin phrases, words and abbreviations form part of the English language: *vice versa, alma mater, et al, habeas corpus, persona non grata, in vino veritas, ipso facto, e.g.,* ignoramus, am and pm, QED, and *carpe diem* are all still commonly used in English today.

▲ *Above: As is the case in many parts of Rome, the night illuminations on the historical Campidoglio are particularly attractive.*

TREATY OF ROME

The original Treaty of Rome, setting up the EEC (European Economic Community) was signed in the **Sale dei Conservatori** (the Apartment of the Conservatori) in 1957 by the six founder member countries (Belgium, France, Germany, Italy, Luxembourg and the Netherlands) – humble beginnings indeed for the emergent superpower today renamed the **European Union**.

IL CAMPIDOGLIO (CAPITOLINE HILL)

There is no better place in Rome to start absorbing the city's ancient history. Just behind the beautifully designed **Piazza del Campidoglio** (a masterpiece by Michelangelo) and its impressive replica of an equestrian bronze of **Marcus Aurelius** is a viewpoint over the entire **Roman Forum**, right down to the Colosseum.

The Campidoglio is surrounded on three sides by majestic palaces restored to Michelangelo's designs but finished only after his death. If you stand with your back to the long **Cordonata** steps leading up to the huge Classical statues of **Castor** and **Pollux** (sons of the Greek god Zeus), which stand sentinel to the Campidoglio, the palace opposite you is the **Palazzo Senatorio**, official office of the Mayor of Rome; on your left is the **Palazzo Nuovo** and, opposite that, the **Palazzo dei Conservatori**. Together, these comprise the **Musei Capitolini** (closed on Mondays), first created in 1471, making this the world's oldest surviving museum. Around the back of the Palazzo Senatorio, you will find one of the finest views over the forum along with a replica of the famous Etruscan statue of a rather emaciated she-wolf suckling **Romulus** and **Remus**. The original, dating from around 500BC, is in the Palazzo dei Conservatori, next door.

Palazzo Nuovo ★★★

Renowned for its collection of Classical sculpture, the Palazzo Nuovo is where you will gain some understanding of the great artistic achievements of both Classical Greece and Ancient Rome. Pope Sixtus IV donated the Lateran bronzes to the people of Rome in 1471; in 1586, Pope Sixtus V added further works and, in 1733, Pope Clement XII donated the Albani collection to form the nucleus of this valuable collection. The Greek works include both originals and Roman copies of Greek statues. Among these are the *Dying Gaul*, *Red Faun*, the so-called *Capitoline Venus* (a true beauty in marble), the **Discobolus**, Greek busts of philosophers and poets, numerous sculptures and mosaics from Hadrian's Villa (Tivoli) and some splendid sarcophagi.

Palazzo Senatorio ★

This is the Mayor of Rome's official seat and is open to the public by special permission only. It bustles with activity as military and civil personages leave and enter, often accompanied by fully uniformed **Carabinieri**. The present palace was redesigned by Michelangelo. Beneath its western façade, on the Campidoglio, is an elaborate fountain flanked by two large Classical sculptures of the Tiber and Nile, with a figure of **Minerva** above.

Palazzo dei Conservatori ★★

This building contains the important Sale dei Conservatori, as well as the Museo del Palazzo dei Conservatori and the Pinacoteca. The **Sale dei Conservatori** (originally the seat of the Conservatori

---

ENGLISH-LANGUAGE BOOKSHOPS

Want a good read in English or some background material on Ancient Rome? Check out the following bookshops, which have both new and second-hand books in English:
• **Feltrinelli**, via VE Orlando 84 (metro: Repubblica) and via del Babuino 39/40.
• **Anglo-American Book Co.**, via della Vite 102, Spagna area.
• **Mel Bookstore**, via Nazionale 254.
• **Almost Corner Bookshop**, via del Moro 45 (Trastevere area), tel: 06 583 6942.
• **Bibli**, via dei Fienaroli 28.

▼ *Below: In the centre of the Campidoglio, Marcus Aurelius rides to victory.*

GAIUS JULIUS CAESAR (100–44BC)

A formidable military man, skilled at commanding his soldiers, Caesar rose to fame during the 1st century BC when he led numerous victorious campaigns intent on enlarging the boundaries of the Roman Republic. In 49BC, and against the orders of the Senate, Caesar led his army across the **Rubicon River** (hence our saying today, 'to cross the Rubicon', meaning to take an irrevocable step) and in 44BC declared himself ruler of the Republic. His supreme position lasted just a month for he was slain on the **Ides of March** (the 15th) 44BC, in a part of Rome that is now know as the **Area Sacra**, a neglected archaeological site populated by mangy cats.

magistrates) is a beautifully decorated series of rooms (take note of the 16th- and 17th-century frescoes), which house the museum's main sculpture collection.

Other treasures within the museum include the colossal head of **Constantine II**, the sublime **Capitoline Venus** dating from the 1st century BC, the **Spinario** bronze of a child removing a thorn from the sole of his foot, and the original statue of equestrian **Marcus Aurelius**, which once stood in the centre of Piazza del Campidoglio.

The **Museo del Palazzo dei Conservatori** has more Classical sculpture, Egyptian and Etruscan items. It shelters the Castellani collection of Etruscan, Greek and Italian items found when excavation of archaeological sites in Lazio and southern Etruria started in the 1860s.

Not to be missed, either, is the **Pinacoteca Capitolina**, an impressive picture gallery founded in 1750, with an enviable collection of paintings from the 14th to 18th centuries. Among the works on display here are paintings by Titian (*Baptism of Christ*), Rubens (*Discovery of Romulus and Remus*), Reni, Pietro da Cortona (*Sacrifice of Polysenna*), Annibale Carracci, Caravaggio (an adolescent *St John the Baptist*), Guercino and Lorenzo Lotto. The Pinacoteca Capitolina also houses a very valuable collection of exquisite 18th- and 19th-century porcelain, including pieces from Asia.

AREA SACRA AND TEATRO DI MARCELLO (MARCELLUS' THEATRE)

Two thousand years ago, in a spot near the bustling **Largo di Torre Argentina** and the attractive **Teatro Argentina**, Julius Caesar was stabbed to death. This 2nd-century BC Roman site is closed to all but the cats and you have to walk through a number of backstreets – an area rarely penetrated by tourists – until you reach the substantial Roman ruin of the **Teatro di Marcello**, a once-fabulous amphitheatre

◀ *Left: The distinctive tower of Santa Maria in Cosmedin locates this Medieval church.*
◀◀ *Opposite: Today not much remains of the Area Sacra in Largo Argentina, but this was once the site of four temples. Closed to the public, the ruins can be observed from the pavement above.*

dating from the 1st decade BC. It was conceived by Julius Caesar but dedicated by Augustus to the memory of his nephew, Marcellus. During the times of the Roman Empire, it was renovated at least a couple of times. Open daily, except Mondays.

Unusually, archaeologists have not made much headway here as parts of the ruins were converted into apartments in the Middle Ages, and are still in the vice-like grip of a private landlord. However, stop and marvel at the edge of the road at the curved walls of this vast amphitheatre and the few remaining columns from the now-ruined **Temple of Apollo**.

While exploring the area between the Area Sacra and the Teatro, be sure to stop at the **Fontana delle Tartarughe** (Fountain of the Tortoises) in Piazza Mattei, a beautiful fountain held aloft by four youths, commissioned by the Mattei family in the 1580s. A century later, an unknown artist (Bernini is suggested) added four tortoises to complete the fountain.

Off the beaten track (and past some rather awful pre-War Fascist architecture) is the **Piazza della Bocca della Verità** on the site of the ancient cattle market of Imperial Rome. Still standing are the remains of the late Republican **Arch of Janus**, two attractive and small temples, both Graeco-Roman in style, as well as the church of **Santa Maria in Cosmedin**, one of Rome's best-preserved Medieval churches.

SANTA MARIA IN COSMEDIN

Renowned for its splendid Medieval mosaics, this ancient church (at Bocca della Verità 18) is smallish, plain and rather dark. Towering above Santa Maria is a tall seven-storey bell tower dating from the church's rebuilding in 1123. The church has unusually thin columns along the nave, wonderful stonework on the floor, a fine Gothic *baldacchino* created by one of the Cosmati sons and, probably its greatest asset, a low-relief sculpted human face set in the wall. Its mouth – a gaping hole, known as the **Bocca della Verità** (Mouth of Truth) – attracts tourists by the hundreds who place their hands inside and pose for photos. Originally, it was used as a 'litmus test' for suspects who believed, if they lied, the mouth would close.

CRYPTA BALBI

Over the last 30 years, there have been extensive excavations around the ancient Teatro di Balbo. The Crypta Balbi (via delle Botteghe Oscura 31, on the northern edge of the Ghetto) is a branch of the Museo Nazionale Romano, a fascinating mix of museum and archaeological site, with an excellent collection of Dark Age material from Rome's lost years, the 5th–10th centuries AD.

THE PROTESTANT CEMETERY

More accurately described as a non-Catholic cemetery – it hosts **Buddhists**, **Orthodox** believers and **atheists** – this cemetery is the last resting place for a number of well-known people who made the city their home. Among these are **Julius Goethe**, son of the writer poet, Romantic poets **Percy Bysshe Shelley**, **John Keats** and **Joseph Severn**, and Scottish surgeon, **John Bell** as well as **Antonio Gramsci**, atheist founder of the Italian Communist Party.

TESTACCIO AND THE CIRCO MASSIMO

Right off the tourist's usual route, the area of **Testaccio** has an interesting history and an unusual monument. The **Monte di Testaccio**, a mound of an archaeological site, owes its being to building rubble and the millions of *amphorae* jettisoned during the Empire. A modern statue at Piazza dell'Emporio commemorates this. Testaccio is, today, a leafy, well-designed neighbourhood of relatively modern city planning. In its midst is the **Mercato di Testaccio**, Piazza Testaccio, a colourful produce market of some reputation. Testaccio is also known for some excellent restaurants and its good nightlife.

Il Piramide di Caius Cestius (Caius Cestius' Pyramid) *

The snowy white form of this marble pyramid (just opposite the Metro Ostiense) sits rather uncomfortably in its modern surrounds. Rising to a height of 27m (90ft), it was built as the tomb of **Caius Cestius**, a wealthy magistrate, after his death in 12BC.

Circo Massimo (Circus Maximus) *

A rickety, old tram takes you from Caius Cestius' Pyramid to the vast, (now) grassy Circus Maximus, once the largest stadium in Ancient Rome and used for chariot races and athletic competitions from the 4th century BC until AD549. It is still used as a jogging track. At the northern end is a small temple to Mithras.

JEWISH ROME

Although Rome is seldom associated with a large Jewish community, Jews have lived in the city for over 2200 years. The rectangular area between the Theatre of Marcellus, along the Via Portico d'Ottavia, down to the Island of Tiberina and bordered by the modern thoroughfare, Via Arenula, was – and, to a large extent, still is – the Jewish area of the capital.

The Ghetto *

In 1555, a decree was passed preventing Jews from living elsewhere in the city, and they were evicted to the area known as the Ghetto. Here they were obliged to attend Christian worship each Sunday at nearby churches. Despite concerted efforts to convert the Jewish community over the centuries, the majority clung to their religion and suffered horribly for it.

In 1848, the Jews were freed of the restricting Ghetto regulations and many homes were torn down in 1888. However, not everything was razed and the area continues to hold traces of its past, including a plaque to the thousand Jews deported in World War II. It still remains a largely Jewish neighbourhood with kosher shops, local bakeries with Jewish pastries, and restaurants specializing in Jewish cuisine.

Fish Market *

At the end of the **Via del Portico d'Ottavia** is part of an ancient rectangular portico, renovated in 23BC and renamed in honour of Octavia (the wife of Mark Anthony). During the 8th century, a church was founded under the elaborate remaining columns of the portico. Later, in the 12th century, part of the portico was incorporated into a fish market and when the church was rebuilt – and further embellished in the 16th century – it was unimaginatively renamed **Sant'Angelo in Pescheria** (St Angelo in the Fishmarket).

◄ *Opposite: The dazzling white, surprising form of the pyramid tomb of Caius Cestius.*
▼ *Below: Built with the stones of both Classical and Medieval Rome, the Via del Portico d'Ottavia leads off the Ghetto, the Jewish area of town.*

IL CAMPIDOGLIO, JEWISH ROME AND CAMPO DE' FIORI

Palazzo Cenci *

Wandering back towards the River Tiber, you will cross the **Piazza delle Cinque Scuole** (Square of the Five Schools), so called for the five synagogues once found there. A few steps away, in the dark backstreets, lies the austere and forbidding façade of Palazzo Cenci. This belonged to the Cenci family, and dates back to the end of the 16th century. The Cencis rose to notoriety because of **Beatrice Cenci** (a Guido Reni portrait of a young woman in Palazzo Barberini is reputed to be Beatrice) who, aided by her brothers and stepmother, killed her tyrannical father. She was executed a year later in 1599.

Synagogue *

On the Lungotevere dei Cenci, overlooking the banks of the River Tiber and on the fringes of the Ghetto, Rome's Synagogue was built at the end of the 1800s, early 1900s. It is an imposing building which is, today, extremely well guarded by uniformed and plain-clothed police officers, affording a reassuring measure of protection for its 15,000 members and the few tourists who come to visit. It has a small museum (open daily, except Saturdays and Jewish holidays) illustrating the long history of Rome's Jewish community.

A TRIP ON THE TIBER

Many of Rome's river banks have been cleaned up and scenic boat rides in vessels akin to Paris' *Bateaux Mouche* are now an interesting alternative, offering a view of the city from another angle. Two companies offer guided cruises:
Battelli di Roma, via della Tribuna Tor de' Spechi 15, tel: 06 9774 5498, www.battellidiroma.it and **Tourvisa Italia**, tel: 06 448 741, www.tourvisa.it

◀ Left: This impressive trompe l'œil corridor, designed by Borromini, is to be found in the courtyard of Palazzo Spada.
◀◀ Opposite: A panoramic view from Piazza Garibaldi takes in the synagogue, Ghetto and the huge monument to Victor Emmanuel II, Il Vittoriano.

THE BEST OF BAROQUE

- **Bernini**, at his best, can be found on the **Tomb of Alexander VII**, the *baldacchino* and colonnade, all at **St Peter's**, the **Fontana dei Quattro Fiumi** in Piazza Navona, the oval church of **Sant'Andrea al Quirinale**, *The Ecstasy of Santa Teresa* in the church of **Santa Maria della Vittoria**, or in various works exhibited in the **Museo Borghese**.
- The greatest work by **Borromini** includes **San Carlo alle Quattro Fontane**, **Palazzo Pamphilj**, and the trompe l'œil corridor in **Palazzo Spada**.
- Talented Baroque painters include the **Carracci** brothers and **Michelangelo Merisi da Caravaggio**. Works by these artists, and many more from the Baroque era, can be found in **Galleria Spada**, **Palazzo Corsini**, **Galleria Doria Pamphilj** and in the **Palazzo dei Conservatori**.

EAST OF VIA ARENULA

Busy Via Arenula marks the boundary of the Jewish neighbourhood. The other side of this bustling thoroughfare takes you back into Renaissance Rome and into an area of orderly civic building. The first large palace you come across, once backing directly onto the Tiber, is the **Palazzo Spada**.

Palazzo Spada and Galleria ★★

For lovers of both Classical sculpture and 17th-century paintings, the Gallery in Palazzo Spada (piazza Capo di Ferro 13) is most rewarding. Although the palace was actually built in the 16th century, it takes it name from **Cardinal Bernardino Spada** who acquired it in the 17th century. Borromini renovated the building for its new owner and added a marvellous trompe l'œil corridor in a small niche area, giving the impression of a long, well-proportioned colonnade.

The Gallery contains many good works, and a few outstanding ones – all exhibited in 17th-century salons. Among the most prized paintings are the portraits by **Guido Reni**, a good copy of Titian's *Paul III*, the Dürer painting of a young man, Guercino's *Death of Dido*, and *The Visitation* by Andrea del Sarto. Closed on Mondays.

IL CAMPIDOGLIO, JEWISH ROME AND CAMPO DE' FIORI

Behind the Palazzo Spada lies the **Ponte Sisto**, commissioned by Pope Sixtus IV (1471–1484). A very attractive pedestrian-only bridge, it leads across the Tiber and into Trastevere. It is a pleasant walk (though there are rarely many pedestrians) along the Lungotevere dei Tebaldi and di Sangallo or, on the opposite bank of the river, along the Lungo-tevere di Farnesina and Janicolense, towards Castel Sant'Angelo.

▲ *Above: One of Rome's most beautiful palazzi, the Palazzo Farnese is, unfortunately, rarely open to visitors. However, you can glimpse its gardens from the Via Giulia.*

Palazzo Farnese **

The French Embassy has, for over three centuries, occupied this beautiful Renaissance palace dominating **Piazza Farnese** which, unless you have business there, is sadly closed to the public.

It was commissioned by Alessandro Farnese (later **Pope Paul III**), and finished according to the designs of Michelangelo after the pope's death. **Annibale Carracci**, an artist from Bologna, was invited to paint the ceilings. He created some of Rome's greatest works, filled with mythological figures placed in a soaring setting. The Farnese also created the piazza in front of the palace so as to give space to view its magnificent façade.

Via Giulia *

Behind Palazzo Farnese and parallel to the Tiber runs Via Giulia, brainchild of Pope Julius II. It still boasts some remarkably impressive, private mansions. Largely occupied by foreign governments (the rents are exorbitant!) or reorganized into smart apartments, Via Giulia is particularly attractive.

PORTA FORTUNA

Romans have an answer for everything! So occupied with admiring Rome's many monuments (or possibly its good-looking citizens!), you might inadvertently put your foot in a canine legacy left on the pavement. *'Porta fortuna!'* your Roman host will exclaim with a laugh – 'It'll bring good luck.' Nothing like looking on the bright side of things!

Originally, Palazzo Farnese was to be connected to Villa Farnese (on the Trastevere side of the Tiber) and work began on the viaduct. Today, all that remains of this project is a small bridge bedecked with hanging vines. Be sure not to miss **Il Mascherone**, a much-loved but particularly strange fountain commissioned by the Farnese and created from a Roman mask and basin.

Sant'Eligio degli Orefici **

It is just a short walk along Via Giulia from Palazzo Farnese to this small but beautiful church, at via de Sant'Eligio 8A. Designed by **Raphael** (though finished by **Peruzzi** after his death), it is built on the form of a Greek cross with a cupola.

Walking along the Via Giulia to the far end, and admiring the various buildings as you stroll, you will come across **San Giovanni dei Fiorentini** near the Piazza del Oro. An imposing 18th-century church façade introduces you to the place of worship for the considerable Florentine community living in 16th-century Rome. Although Antonio da Sangallo began the work, it was Carlo Maderno who finished it in 1614. With understandable nepotism, the church is largely decorated by Florentine artists. Of interest to Baroque aficionados is the fact that both **Maderno** and **Francesco Borromini** are buried in the church.

GLADIATOR

Ridley Scott brought the world of the Roman Empire to the fore in a very realistic epic film, *Gladiator*, based on the revenge of an ex-general from the Roman army who, in around 160AD, fights for his life in the Colosseum. However, the real-life look of **Classical Rome** was in fact recreated in the special effects studios of London's Soho.

▼ *Below: Antiquity and Renaissance art combine in this odd-looking fountain, Il Mascherone, the Big Mask.*

CORSO VITTORIO EMANUELE

Corso Vittorio Emanuele runs from the Tiber to Largo di Torre Argentina where it joins the Via dei Plebiscito and continues onward to Piazza Venezia, thus creating one of the most important routes across central Rome. Along its west–east axis there are a number of

CHIESA NUOVA

Chiesa Nuova, or Santa Maria in Vallicella – to give it its correct name – is an interesting building on **Piazza Chiesa Nuova**, attached to the **Oratorio dei Filippini**. Their brilliant white façades shine out through the polluted surrounds. Built as the centre of **Filippo Neri's** new order, the **Fathers of the Oratory**, the church is beautifully gilded and decorated with some excellent works by, among others, **Pietro da Cortona** and Rubens. Neri organized *oratori* (musical get-togethers) here, and the word *oratorio* is now applied to a musical art form, the religious opera, which grew out of these gatherings.

▶ *Opposite: Early risers get the pick of the crop in Campo de' Fiori's market.*
▼ *Below: The so-called Chiesa Nuova, Santa Maria in Vallicella, and Filippo Neri's Oratory.*

notable buildings, including **Chiesa Nuova**, **Palazzo della Cancelleria**, the **Museo Barracco**, **San Andrea della Valle**, **Chiesa del Gesù** (*see* page 53), the **Palazzo Doria Pamphilj** (*see* page 68) and **Palazzo Venezia** (*see* page 52).

Palazzo della Cancelleria *

Just off the northern side of Campo de' Fiori, on Piazza della Cancelleria, is the massive, near-white Palazzo della Cancelleria. A beautiful palace built for **Cardinal Raffaello Riario** in the late 1480s, it positively glistens in the bright sun. Although the architect of this fine palace remains unknown, its design marks a distinct turning point in the history of architecture. The High Renaissance was born from this moment and the architectural glories of Italy belonged ever-increasingly to Rome, not Florence. Sadly, the beautiful courtyard is marred by the presence of parked cars, an all-too-frequent occurrence in central Rome.

Palazzo Piccolo Farnesina (Museo Barracco) *

Just around the corner from Piazza della Cancelleria, at Corso Vittorio Emanuele II 166, is a tiny but elegant palazzo much in need of cleaning and restoration. It was built in 1523 for Thomas Le Roy, a French prelate; today, it houses the **Museo Barracco**, a collection of Classical sculpture. There are not many exhibits but, as the works were part of the personal collection of Senator Giovanni Barracco before they were donated to the municipality of Rome, they are of high quality. Among the politician's collection are some valuable Assyrian works in bronze and terracotta, Egyptian bas-reliefs and busts, Greek heads, female figures and athletes, and some pieces from Imperial Rome. There is also space for temporary art exhibits. Closed on Mondays.

Piazza Campo de' Fiori **

One of the older parts of Rome, hidden in a maze of narrow, winding streets, lies the popular 'square', Piazza Campo de' Fiori. An elongated piazza that was once a meadow (hence its name, 'Field of Flowers') and then one of Rome's most important squares, it is known today for its brightly coloured **morning market** (the mosaic of colourful, clean vegetables, flowers and fruit is a wonderful sight), has a peaceful laid-back air about it and, despite the number of tourists, breathes 'Real Rome'.

A central position in the square is occupied by the brooding statue of a hooded **Giordano Bruno**, a 'heretic' burned alive by the Inquisition in 1600 – a sobering reminder that this was the site where many others lost their lives.

Campo de' Fiori is largely pedestrian (although not off-limits to motorbikes). On Sundays and weekday afternoons – when the market has closed – Campo de' Fiori provides a fine place to stroll, stop for a *cappuccino* or *aperitivo*, or linger over a leisurely pasta lunch or dinner. In the small streets on each side of the piazza, there are scores of cafés, restaurants and popular *trattorie*; the shops here have a genuine neighbourhood quality to them and prices are much more realistic than those in the most popular tourist spots.

ROME IN FILM

Rome has inspired many a film from the big film studios of the 20th century. An early epic, MGM's *Ben Hur: A Tale of Christ* was made in 1926; Cecil B. de Mille made *The Ten Commandments* in 1923. *Cleopatra* was made in 1934 with Claudette Colbert and again in 1963 with Elizabeth Taylor. *Quo Vadis?* was made in 1951, *Ben Hur* in 1959 – the same year that Richard Burton starred in *The Robe*; this was followed by *Spartacus* in 1960. Anthony Mann's *Fall of the Roman Empire* marked the end of the era and Rome, as a subject, fell out of vogue until Ridley Scott's *Gladiator* in 2000 (*see* panel, page 63). Latterly the 2009 movie *Angels and Demons* was also filmed in the city. Film crews still use the streets for local movies, commercials and TV soaps.

5. The Pantheon, Parliament and Piazza Navona

Both the Pantheon and Piazza Navona belong to the Imperial era of Roman history. The Pantheon is one of the city's best-preserved Classical monuments and still impresses even the most jaded of sightseers. Every day thousands of foot-weary visitors stop in the **Piazza Rotonda** to contemplate this extraordinary building over a cup of hot coffee or an overpriced meal. It sits fairly incongruously in a neighbourhood of narrow streets which, thankfully, have now been declared off-limits to cars.

Though the palaces that surround the elongated oval of Piazza Navona date from the 16th century, the form of the piazza replicates the outline of the original **Stadium of Domitian**, which once stood on this site. Together with the lacy network of streets linking these two great landmarks, they form a solid foundation on which 2000 years of history have been constructed. To wander through these streets is to walk back through the pages of the city's history.

Strolling away from **Piazza Navona** the atmosphere of Ancient Rome metamorphoses into that of Baroque Rome: imposing buildings and elaborate façades are decorated by exuberantly frilly and extraneous architectural details. **Sant'Ignazio** is a fine example of this, a church built for the Jesuits, while the large **Palazzo di Montecitorio**, solid and magisterial, houses Italy's parliament. The area's restaurants and *trattorie* are patronized by politicians and barons of industry and, infrequently, by tourists.

Villa Borghese
Città del Vaticano
Stazione Centrale
Roma Termini
Quirinale
Trastevere
Testaccio

DON'T MISS

*** **The Pantheon:** visit in the afternoon or early morning.
*** **Palazzo Doria Pamphilj:** a leisurely visit through the elaborate rooms.
*** **Piazza Navona:** eat lunch and take an afternoon stroll in the elegant piazza.
** **Santa Maria Sopra Minerva:** a medieval church built on the ruins of the Temple of Minerva.
* **Giolitti:** indulge yourself with a *gelato* (ice cream).

◄ *Opposite: The interior of the Pantheon incorporates architecture from many different eras.*

67

VIA DEL CORSO

This main thoroughfare is thankfully now largely closed to traffic. It runs from Piazza del Popolo to Piazza Venezia, and is one of the city's main shopping streets. Paying tribute to the great German poet is the **Casa di Goethe** (Goethe's House; via del Corso 18) a small museum in the actual rooms in which he stayed with his painter friend, Tischbein, when he came to Rome in 1786–88. Among the items on display are rare manuscripts, illustrated texts and various first editions. Closed on Tuesdays.

The **Museo del Corso**, via del Corso 320, is an exhibition space housed in an old palace, offering a variety of temporary art and historic exhibitions. Closed on Mondays.

Palazzo Doria Pamphilj ***

▲ *Above: Palazzo Doria Pamphilj is still owned by the Doria Pamphilj family.*
▶ *Opposite: An unusual concave façade dominates Piazza San Ignazio.*

One of Rome's most important art galleries, the **Doria Pamphilj Collection** (piazza del Collegio Romano 2) is a privately owned gallery of paintings and sculpture accumulated by two great families who intermarried. Their story is told on the portable information cassettes, narrated by the current prince. Closed on Thursdays.

Among the many paintings that crowd the walls are some real masterpieces, but don't just gaze at the exhibits: the various salons and the chapel are wonderful works of art too.

Be sure to look out for **Velázquez's** portrait of *Innocent X* (a member of the Pamphilj family), landscapes by **Claude Lorrain**, religious subjects by **Annibale Carracci**, two **Caravaggio** paintings – *Rest on the Flight into Egypt*, with its striking back view of the angel musician, and *The Penitent*

Map

Pantheon to Piazza Navona

0 ___ 200 m
0 ___ 200 yd

Via del Coronari, Via dei Coronari, S. Antonio d. Portoghesi, Via Prefetti, Via dell' Orso, Via della Scrofa, S. Agostino, HOTEL RAPHAEL, Via Coppelle, Via Maddalena, VIA GIUSTINIANI, Corso del Rinascimento, Via dell'Anima, Piazza Navona, Palazzo Madama, S. Eustachio, S. Maria della Rotonda, Pantheon, VIA D. PASTINI, Piazza d. Rotunda, S. Ignazio, S. Maria Minerva, Piazza della Minerva, Via Seminario, Collegio Romano, Piazza del Parlamento, Piazza S. Silvestro, Colonna, Camera d. Deputati, Palazzo Chigi, Galleria Colonna, Piazza di Montecitorio, Piazza Colonna, Piazza di Pietro, Via del Corso, Palacio del Governo Vecchio, Palazzo Pamphilj, PENSIONE NAVONA, Via Montserone, Via Monterone, Pigna, Piazza Collegio Romano, Palazzo Doria Pamphilj, Palazzo Braschi, Palacio della Cancelleria, Teatro Valle, Palazzo Massimo, Piazza Grazioli, Palazzo Altieri, Piazza del Gesù, Via Cappellari, Via del Pellegrino, Piazza Campo de' Fiori, S. Andrea della Valle, Corso Vittorio Emanuele II, Palazzo Vidoni, Via d. Plebiscito, S. Marco

Magdalene, echoing the pose of Mary in the previous painting – a *Deposition* by **Hans Memlinc**, and various paintings by the Dutch master, **Jan Brueghel the Elder**. There are also some **Gobelin** tapestries.

Wander onwards, through the **Piazza del Collegio Romano**, and beyond the **Palazzo del Collegio Romano**, which was formerly the site of a Jesuit college. Take the Via Sant'Ignazio to the piazza of the same name.

Piazza Sant'Ignazio *

Dominating this delightful piazza is the Jesuit church of Sant'Ignazio (St Ignatius), one of Rome's most lavish. It has an extraordinary trompe l'œil ceiling, painted by Andrea Pozzo, which even goes as far as to deceive the observer into believing – if you stand at the appropriate spot – that there is a frescoed cupola above.

The piazza is, however, also noteworthy. Its sienna-coloured buildings, many of which have been renovated, and the lavish concave façade on the palace opposite, contribute to a theatrical atmosphere where summer concerts have been staged.

PIAZZA COLONNA

A beautiful piazza dominated by a fine marble column, Piazza Colonna is the site of the magnificent **Palazzo Chigi**, built at the end of the 16th century by the Aldobrandini family and now the prime minister's official residence. Dwarfed along the opposite side of the piazza is the pretty church of **Santa Maria in Via Lata**, but pride of place goes to the imposing column dedicated to **Marcus Aurelius**. Approximately 40m (140ft) high, it is carved in a scroll fashion with beautifully executed bas-relief scenes depicting Marcus Aurelius' victories and dates from AD180–196.

Piazza di Montecitorio *

To the west of Piazza Colonna, another large sloping 'square' with an ancient Egyptian obelisk faces the Palazzo di Montecitorio, seat of the Italian parliament. Remodelled on a 16th-century palace designed for Innocent X by Bernini, it was converted to its parliamentary function in the early part of the 20th century. The Palazzo di Montecitorio has an unusual convex façade – another ingenious device by Bernini – that shows it to its best advantage.

Wandering from Piazza di Montecitorio through the backstreets towards Piazza Rotonda, you will suddenly come upon **Piazza di Pietra** and Italy's stock exchange, **La Borsa**, which is incorporated into a historic monument, **Il Templo di Adriano** (Temple of Hadrian). Built by his son in AD145 in memory of his father, by then a god, its beautiful Corinthian columns form part of the façade of today's stock exchange.

HADRIAN'S TEMPLE

In accordance with current Roman practice, the wisest Roman emperors were deified after death. Such was the case of **Hadrian** to whom this temple was posthumously dedicated by his son, **Antoninus Pius**. To get a better idea of how this elegant temple must have looked, a scale model is shown in a window on the opposite side of the piazza.

▶ Right: Filippino Lippi's magnificent altarpiece depicting St Thomas Aquinas presenting Cardinal Carafa to the Virgin, part of the Carafa chapel in Santa Maria sopra Minerva.

PIAZZA DELLA MINERVA

If you backtrack through Via Sant'Ignazio and along Via Pie d' Marmo – where a large Roman foot is the highlight – you will arrive in Piazza della Minerva. With an obelisk borne on the back of an elaborately carved marble elephant (a Bernini folly), the mostly pedestrian square is dominated on one side by the church of **Santa Maria sopra Minerva**.

Santa Maria sopra Minerva **

An old church of immense artistic interest, Santa Maria sopra Minerva has a rather dreary façade but the interior of the church is a delight. Its restoration has, to some people's taste, over-emphasized the gilt and colour but the effect is nevertheless impressive. Be sure to look up at the star-studded blue ceiling, and note how the light streams through the clerestory windows to pattern the lovely marble floor.

Two side chapels deserve a visit: the **Cappella Carafa**, donated by Cardinal Olivieri Carafa and decorated with frescoes and paintings by Florentine artist, **Filippino Lippi**, and the chapel designed by **Carlo Maderno**, with an altarpiece of *The Annunciation* by Antoniazzo Romano. There is also a fresco by Merlozzo da Forlì on the opposite side of the church.

PIAZZA ROTONDA

Street signs from Piazza Navona, Via del Corso and Corso Vittorio Emanuele II lead the visitor through narrow, dark streets into the Piazza Rotonda, home of the **Pantheon**. The sloping piazza is rimmed with cafés and restaurants, all offering outside seating, colourful parasols and views of the 16 granite Corinthian columns that form the Pantheon's Classical façade.

▲ *Above: The convex façade of the huge Palazzo di Montecitorio, now the seat of Italy's parliament.*

▶ Right: The beautifully proportioned façade of the Pantheon is the focal point for many tourists taking a breather over coffee or cocktails.

The Pantheon ★★★

One of Rome's most extraordinary buildings, the Pantheon (which in Greek means 'all the gods') has been a place of worship for some 2000 years. It was originally constructed by **Marcus Agrippa** around 27BC as a temple of pagan worship but was later destroyed by fire and replaced by Hadrian, the great emperor-architect. But, at the beginning of the 7th century, it was consecrated by Pope Bonifacio IV as a place of Christian worship and has remained so to this day.

Circular, with a coffered dome, the magnificent Pantheon rises to a height of 43.3m (142ft) and is the same height as the width of the building – in fact, a vertical section of its plan forms a perfect circle. In the centre of the dome, an oculus of some nine metres (30ft) remains open to the elements. Sunlight streams in during summer, illuminating the multi-coloured marble floor and elegant lower walls, while showers fall unhindered in winter.

Around the walls are four tombs of note, those of Italy's first king, **Vittorio Emanuele II**, his queen, **Margherita**, Baroque violinist and composer **Arcangelo Corelli**, and the artist, **Raphael**, who requested his interment in the building. Open daily.

FETTUCCINE AL ALFREDO

One of Italy's great pasta dishes, glorified by the likes of **Douglas Fairbanks** and **Mary Pickford**, is Fettuccine al Alfredo. It was invented in 1925 by owner-chef **Alfredo**, of the famous **Alfredo alla Scrofa** restaurant, via della Scrofa 104. Although the recipe remains a house secret, home-made *fettuccine* ribbon noodles are served on a specially heated plate coated in Alfredo's sauce of pure butter, finest parmigiano and … he's keeping mum about the rest of the ingredients.

AROUND PIAZZA NAVONA

Focal point for Romans and visitors alike, the unusually shaped Piazza Navona has a wealth of pretty outdoor cafés and restaurants, homogenous Baroque architecture and a number of interesting sights in the vicinity.

Piazza Navona ★★★

Once the **Stadium of Domitian**, this elegant, elongated 'square' is one of Rome's favourite places for relaxation, dining and people-watching. The 16th-century palaces rising from the perimeter of the piazza were constructed around the central part of the stadium and comprise some extremely impressive buildings, many of which have been recently renovated.

But it is the fountains that hold the focus of this piazza. Pride of place goes to the central **Fontana dei Quattro Fiumi**, commissioned by Innocent X (whose Palazzo Pamphilj occupies a large frontage nearby). It is a gushing fountain surrounding an Egyptian obelisk and, with its colossal statues, fêtes the four greatest rivers known at that time – the Danube, Ganges, Nile and Plate. Bernini designed this Baroque splendour with characteristic vigour and it was completed by his assistants in 1651. At the southern end of the piazza is the **Fontana del Moro** by Giacomo della Porta and, at the northern end, the **Fontana di Nettuno**, where Neptune struggles with a recalcitrant monster of the deep amid a turbulence of sea horses, is by Antonio della Bitta.

▼ Below: The centre of the Baroque Fontana di Nettuno, Piazza Navona.

WHERE TO BUY ANTIQUES

The narrow streets filtering into old Rome on the western side of **Piazza Navona** form a neighbourhood little frequented by visitors. There are, however, some excellent restaurants here, and also a wealth of small, local shops and antique dealers – pedestrian-only **Via Coronari**, with its lovely old buildings, is the scene of Rome's annual antiques fair, while **Piazza Fontanella Borghese** daily offers books, prints and small *objets*.

Palazzo Pamphilj *

Built for Innocent X, a Pamphilj pope, this huge palace was designed by **Girolamo Rainaldi** and **Borromini** while **Pietro da Cortona** was responsible for some of the magnificent frescoes inside. It is nowadays occupied by the Brazilian Embassy and members of the public are not allowed inside unless they obtain prior permission. Alongside the palace is another Borromini building, the church of Sant'Agnese.

Sant'Agnese in Agone *

St Agnese was indeed in agony, but the *agone* in the name of this church refers to the athletic contests, the *agones* held in Domitian's stadium. Beatified for miraculously defying death and public shame, Agnes was finally executed in AD304 by Diocletian and lies buried in the **Catacombs of St Agnes** in the **Basilica di Sant'Agnese fuori le Mura**. This small church was started by the Rainaldi father-and-son team and finished by Borromini, who also added the concave façade.

Palazzo Braschi (Museo di Roma) *

With a strange triangular shape, the Palazzo Braschi forms the southern corner of Piazza Navona and opens onto Piazza San Pantaleo 10, on the other side. It was erected by Pope Pius VI Braschi between 1791 and 1798 and houses the **Museo di Roma**, a veritable collection of over 40,000 items documenting ordinary life and traditions from the Middle Ages to the present. Among the exhibits are ceramics, paintings of historical events and banquets, plaster casts executed by 19th-century sculptor Pietro Tenerani, railway carriages used by Pope Pius IX, and various sculptures unearthed during demolition and excavation in the 20th century. Closed on Mondays.

Palazzo Altemps *

Just off the other end of the piazza, in piazza Sant'Apollinaire, the Palazzo Altemps is a stunning 15th-16th century palace, set around an elegant courtyard, now lovingly restored as part of the Museo Nazionale Romano. It contains a wide array of ancient Roman statuary, some, collected by 17th-century Cardinal Ludovisi, from the private residence of Julius Caesar. Closed on Mondays.

SANTA MARIA DELLA PACE AND BEYOND

Behind Piazza Navona, at Vicolo del Arco della Pace 5, lies this small but beautiful church built in the 1480s to thank the Virgin for delivering an end to the war with Turkey; hence its name, Santa Maria della Pace (St Mary of the Peace). **Donato Bramante** added a cloister in 1504 and, under Pope Alexander VII, **Pietro da Cortona** designed and built a lovely semi-circular portico 150 years later.

Not two minutes away, at via della Pace 24, is another church, used by the German community in Rome. **Santa Maria dell'Anima** has a rather dark interior that hides its wealth of detail. Pope Adrian VI is buried in a magnificent tomb designed by **Baldassarre Peruzzi**, and completed after the pope's death in 1523.

Near the banks of the Tiber, and opposite the beautiful **Palazzo di Giustizia**, is the **Museo Napoleonico**, piazza di Ponte Umberto 1. This collection, most of which came from descendants of the Bonaparte family, was donated by Count Giuseppe Primoli. It comprises miniatures, jewels, furniture and court clothing belonging to the Bonapartes. Closed on Mondays.

▲ *Above left: Part of a big renovation project, a restorer paints imitation marble on wood, in Sant'Agnese in Agone, Piazza Navona.*
◄ *Opposite: Piazza Navona is a good place to buy original watercolours of Rome and the Roman countryside.*

HANDMADE SHOES

Italians know their leather and a pair of Italian shoes are worth treasuring. Off the peg **Tods** and **Gucci** have first-class reputations, but the long-standing **Petrocchi** (via dell'Orso 25, tel: 06 687 6289) offers handmade and ready-made shoes. Count on a minimum of $700 and allow 2–3 weeks for the manufacture of your shoes. Shoes can either be collected or mailed home. Clients can always have their shoes reconditioned free of charge at a later date – it's all part of the after-sales service.

6. Piazza di Spagna and Piazza del Popolo

This chic part of town is a focal point for leisure. It bristles with outlets for designer shopping, fashionable boutiques, small but trendy *trattorie* and restaurants, and intimate but luxurious hotels. This is an excellent address from which to explore central Rome on foot. The area also abuts the centrally located public park, **Villa Borghese** with its world-class museum, and adjoins the semi-formal park, **Giardini Pincio** (the Pincio Gardens).

This part of Rome has been popular for some 400 years since the first Spanish ambassador to the Vatican took up residence in the **Piazza di Spagna** and the area around this piazza was considered more or less Spanish territory. Travellers making their way to the Basilica of St Peter's would lodge in this area from whence the walk to the Vatican, through the **Porta del Popolo** – gateway to the Piazza del Popolo – was not long.

The French built the famous **Scalinata della Trinità dei Monti**, the Spanish Steps, which sweep the eye upwards from the piazza to the equally attractive French Baroque church, the **Trinità dei Monti**. The Steps are perhaps the most popular meeting place for travellers in Rome, and have been since the days of the Romantic poets, some of whom lived here.

Radiating westwards from the **Piazza di Spagna** are three streets that spell *alta moda* – the most elite fashion designers in Italy are all to be found here.

Piazza del Popolo is known for its three churches, the most impressive of which is **Santa Maria del Popolo** and, latterly, as a venue for evening spectacles.

DON'T MISS

*** **Ara Pacis:** monument to Peace from Ancient Rome.
*** **Piazza di Spagna:** climb the famed Spanish Steps.
** **Piazza Trinità** and **Giardini Pincio:** magnificent views of Rome.
** **Via Condotti:** take a stroll, and don't forget your credit cards.
** **Café Greco:** enjoy a coffee or an *aperitivo*.
* **Santa Maria del Popolo** and **Trinità dei Monti:** impressive paintings in both.

◀ *Opposite: Seen from the ultra-chic Via Condotti, the twin towers of the Trinità dei Monti provide a magnificent backdrop.*

Piazza di Spagna to Piazza del Popolo

▲ Above: Officers of the Carabinieri, mounted on horseback, are a familiar sight in Rome.
▼ Below: It was Bernini who designed this unusual fountain located in the Piazza di Spagna.

PIAZZA DI SPAGNA

One of the most famous tourist spots in Rome, the largely pedestrian piazza and the flight of steps behind it are named after the 17th-century Palazzo di Spagna, which is the residence of the Spanish Ambassador to the Vatican located on the west side of the piazza, and indeed notable for being the first permanent ambassadorial residence in Rome.

The Spanish Steps ★★★

This lovely piazza not only offers beautiful Roman buildings and a boat-shaped fountain designed by Bernini, but a magnificent sweep of 137 stairs, the **Scalinata della Trinità dei Monti**, leading up to an attractive Baroque church, **Trinità dei Monti**.

On each side of the Spanish Steps, small apartments with matchbox terraces and exuberant little gardens jostle for space. Horses and buggies, flower sellers and milling visitors from all parts of the world kindle a festive, cosmopolitan atmosphere. The beauty of this part of Rome was not lost on travellers – artists and writers in the 18th and 19th centuries and many foreigners made it their temporary home.

Keats-Shelley Memorial House *

At the bottom of the Spanish Steps, piazza di Spagna 26, is this small museum dedicated to the memorabilia and times of **John Keats**, his painter friend **Joseph Severn**, **Percy Shelley**, **Lord Byron** and **Leigh Hunt**, all of whom lived part of their lives in Rome. Keats, in fact, came out to Rome to convalesce but, rather than recovering from tuberculosis, died in this attractive pink building just three months later, in 1826. The *pensione* was acquired at the beginning of the 20th century and opened its doors as a museum in 1909. Among the exhibits are many leather-bound volumes, various manuscripts and autographed letters, a lock of Keats' hair and his death mask. Closed on Sundays.

Trinità dei Monti *

The twin-towered church of Trinità dei Monti commands a magnificent position overlooking southwest Rome. It is an attractive, late 15th-century building with an unusual, double stairway leading into it, and was originally built for the **Convent of the Minims** by Louis XII, though restored some 300 years later. Among the points of interest here are the (rather sombre) side chapels decorated with Mannerist works. Take a look at the two paintings by **Daniele da Volterra**: *The Assumption* is a real masterpiece.

In front of the Trinità dei Monti is the piazza of the same name. Apart from the great views westwards over Piazza di Spagna, it is a focal point for artists, and if the paintings of Roman streets and the *Campagna* don't take your fancy, you can pose for a quick caricature or portrait in charcoal.

Situated to the right of the church, at via Trinità dei Monti 6, is one of Rome's most historic hotels, the **Hotel Hassler Villa Medici**, the privately owned home-from-home for smart visitors since 1885.

BABINGTON'S TEA ROOMS

It is rather incongruous in a city noted for pasta and martinis, but it nevertheless does a brisk trade. Babington's Tea Rooms, at the bottom of the **Spanish Steps**, are a 19th-century institution set up to cater for the needs of the English travellers over a century ago. An old-fashioned, genteel atmosphere still pervades the establishment and although the menu has a few concessions to contemporary tastes, it largely reflects the appetites of its first patrons.

▼ Below: Piazza dei Trinità is a good place to have a personal portrait painted or created out of pastels.

▲ Above: Via Condotti is known for its pricey shops.

▶ Opposite: The fine details sculpted on the Ara Pacis.

VIA FRATTINI, VIA BORGOGNONA AND VIA CONDOTTI

If there is one area dedicated to shopping and the purchase of all that is *alta moda*, it is this zone between Via del Corso and Piazza di Spagna. The names of the streets are synonyms for high fashion – Via Frattini, Via Borgognona and Via Condotti – and if you want to gauge the state of Italian fashion, this is the best place to indulge yourself.

Milling between the different stores, *caffès* and restaurants are the best-dressed women (and men) in Rome, toting designer shopping bags and mobile phones, as well as motley-clad tourists strolling from one fine window display to the next.

The names that made Italy so big on the fashion scene – **Armani**, **Benetton**, **Gucci**, **Laura Biagiotti**, **Fendi**, **Valentino** and **Versace** – may all be found in this golden rectangle. In their midst is **Modigliani**, known for its superb collection of household ware, with a fine range of porcelain and glass from the world's best producers.

Crossing this area, northwest to southeast, are three beautiful small streets of warmly coloured buildings: the flower-filled **Via Mario dei Fiori**, pedestrian-only **Via Bocca di Leone** – with its small street market favoured by smart locals – and **Via Belsiana**. Here you will discover some excellent little restaurants and *trattorie*, specialty shops and some small but distinguished hotels.

To the west of Piazza di Spagna, **Via del Babuino** – noted for its fashion and household goods – links the piazza with **Piazza del Popolo**, slicing through the neighbourhood known as **Campo Marzo**. Parallel, the **Via Margutta** – renowned for its antiques and galleries – branches off. Sandwiched between palaces of deep sienna, it is a very attractive and tranquil side street.

Along the banks of the Tiber, and in an area forgotten by commerce and the world of fashion, lies the ruined **Mausoleo di Augusto** (Augustus' Mausoleum) and **Ara**

Pacis, one of the great legacies of Ancient Rome. Magnificent on its completion in 28BC, Augustus' circular mausoleum today remains as a weed-covered mound, surrounded by funereal cypress trees, and is mainly used by local dogs and joggers. Access to the monument itself is by appointment only.

Ara Pacis (Altar of Peace) ***

The Ara Pacis (Altar of Peace) on Via di Ripetta, has been reconstructed, renovated and enclosed in a glassy new museum designed by Richard Meier. Its solid white marble form positively glistens. The monument was erected in AD13 to commemorate the peace Rome enjoyed as a result of Augustus' successful incorporation of Gaul and Spain into the Empire. It comprises three walls on a dais, reached by a flight of steps, enclosing an altar used annually for an anniversary sacrifice. All the external walls are carved with decorative foliage, and exquisite and extraordinarily lifelike scenes of people, including an array of members of the emperor's family – it has, in today's terms, the realism of a family photograph. Closed on Mondays.

PIAZZA DEL POPOLO

One of Rome's largest cobblestone squares, the Piazza del Popolo is a vast open space with an Egyptian obelisk surrounded by four fountains in its midst. The piazza has changed form various times over the centuries, but owes its present layout to **Giuseppe Valadier**, who incorporated the obelisk into the fountains at the beginning of the 19th century and also laid out the **Pincio Gardens** (see page 83). From the piazza, roads radiate

TWO SANTA MARIAS

The pretty **Santa Maria dei Miracoli** and **Santa Maria in Montesanto** churches were designed by **Carlo Rainaldi** in the second half of the 17th century, but later modified by **Bernini** and **Fontana**. Although they appear to be identical, the sites provided for the two churches were not the same size and so, rather than compromise his design, Rainaldi gave Santa Maria in Montesanto (on the left, when standing in Piazza del Popolo) an oval dome instead of the round one in Santa Maria dei Miracoli. The illusion works well from the centre of the piazza.

▼ *Below: The Baroque façade of Santa Maria dei Miracoli, Piazza del Popolo.*

outward to nearby Piazza di Spagna, Piazza Venezia and through the Pincio Gardens to Villa Borghese. Today, Piazza del Popolo is sometimes used for large open-air shows as its surrounding buildings and solid walls give it an amphitheatre-like ambience.

Along the piazza's southwestern edge are a number of fashionable cafés and restaurants such as the long-standing Rosati. Nearby, and separated by Via del Corso, are the attractive twin Baroque churches of **Santa Maria dei Miracoli** and **Santa Maria in Montesanto**.

Santa Maria del Popolo *

One of Rome's famous churches, Santa Maria del Popolo is one of the less visible churches in this large square, but behind its brick façade are some master-pieces of Renaissance and Baroque art. It was largely rebuilt by Sixtus IV in the 1470s.

Pinturicchio (and his school of followers) created the marvellous frescoes in the **Della Rovere Chapel** and in the apse; **Raphael** was responsible for the tomb, sculpture and painting for the **Chigi Chapel**; **Caravaggio** completed the two paintings of St Peter in the **Caravasi Chapel**, and **Annibale Carracci** painted an altarpiece, *The Assumption*

of the Virgin, and frescoes above it. **Bramante** designed the apse while **Bernini** produced a number of sculptures, the renovation of the interior and finished the Chigi Chapel for banker, Agostino Chigi, after Raphael's death. Give the church sufficient time, for there are many chapels and corners to discover.

Giardini Pincio (Pincio Gardens) **

The beautiful Pincio Gardens overlooking western Rome were designed by **Valadier** at the beginning of the 19th century. Rising on a mound behind Piazza del Popolo, these pleasant gardens are laid out with formal avenues of huge shady trees, statues of illustrious Italians and the ever-present fountains. The gardens are a favourite place for children to let off steam (under the watchful eyes of their foreign nannies or ageing grannies), for tourists to admire the panoramic views, and for Romans to stroll in early evening.

Villa Medici *

It is a pleasant walk through the Giardini Pincio, or a stroll along from Piazza Trinitá, to the beautiful Villa Medici, the site of the French Academy in Rome since 1803. The Academy was set up by Louis XIV in 1666 to give talented painters (and later musicians) a chance to study the Classics. Despite passing through various hands, it retains the name of its 16th-century owner, **Cardinal Ferdinando de' Medici**.

▼ *Below: A moment of relaxation in the lovely Pincio Gardens.*

7
Vatican City

The world's smallest state, **La Città del Vaticano** is completely surrounded by the capital of an entirely different country – a unique situation, but one the Vatican City has learned to live with since Mussolini accorded it sovereignty under the **Lateran Treaty** in 1929. The first buildings in the area that is now known as the Vatican City were erected over St Peter's tomb at the end of the 1st century AD.

The Vatican City we see today owes its appearance to the vision of popes such as Martin V, Nicholas V, Julius II, Paul III and Alexander VII who metamorphosed not just the pontifical territory, but much of the face of a capital that had fallen into decline at the end of the first millennium and who had, by the late 17th century, transformed it into a city of considerable beauty.

There is a resident population of under 1000 living in the Vatican, but there is also a huge transient population of religious personnel. The Vatican City has its own media and postal services but relies almost entirely on tourism for its revenues. Although a city, the gardens, which have been modified by successive popes, provide a remarkably tranquil hideaway in its midst.

The Vatican has not only its own daily newspaper, *l'Osservatore Romano*, but a postal service with its own stamps, **Radio Vaticano** which broadcasts in over 20 languages, and a publishing press. It also has a railway station – now the **Philatelic Museum** (the line runs a distance of just 670m/733yd). The Pope does not have his own transport, relying instead on the Italian military.

Villa Borghese
Città del Vaticano
Stazione Centrale Roma Termini
Quirinale
Trastevere
Testaccio

DON'T MISS

*** St Peter's: enjoy the view from the dome and see Michelangelo's *Pietà*.
*** The Sistine Chapel: see Michelangelo's marvellous historic frescoes.
** The Raphael Rooms: frescoed by Raphael and his followers.
** The Pinacoteca: a fine art gallery.
** Vatican Museums: Roman and Greek sculpture.
* Vatican Gardens: take a walking tour.

◄ *Opposite: This large bronze pine cone lends its name to the Cortile della Pigna at the Vatican Palace.*

BASILICA E PIAZZA DI SAN PIETRO (ST PETER'S BASILICA AND SQUARE)

The largest basilica in Christendom with a magnificent colonnaded piazza in front, St Peter's is undoubtedly one of the most impressive sights in Italy. It is not, however, the mother church of the faith; that title is reserved by San Giovanni in Laterano. The façade of St Peter's is best admired from the 20th-century thoroughfare – the **Via della Conciliazione** – leading to the Tiber, while the views of Rome and the piazza are breathtaking from the bird's-eye viewpoint, high up outside St Peter's dome.

A basilica was first erected by Constantine in the mid-4th century AD on the spot where St Peter was buried. Most of the basilica, however, is the result of Julius II's commissioning **Bramante** as architect in 1503 to redesign the edifice, and the building's subsequent continuation under **Michelangelo** in the mid-16th century. He was responsible for the dome and the rear of the basilica, and in 1626 **Maderno** added a nave and façade. The postscript, the piazza – its circular form taken from Nero and Caligula's circus, which lies beneath – was the brainchild of **Bernini**, whose finishing touches were only completed between 1656 and 1667. It is a wonder that with such a number of artists and the length of time taken to complete it, the building achieves such majesty and harmony.

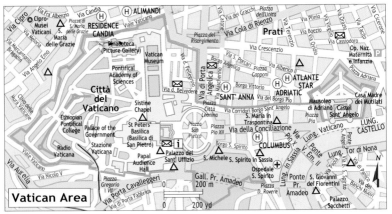

Vatican Area

Not to be missed in the basilica are Michelangelo's intriguingly delicate *Pietà*, now behind protective glass; Bernini's **baldacchino**, made from bronze stripped from the pantheon, its barley-sugar columns sheltering the high altar used by the pope – and only the pope – to celebrate mass; and high above, the light, airy and beautifully decorated dome designed by Michelangelo but finished only after his death. Below the Basilica there are the crypts, with the **Tomb of St Peter**.

▲ *Above: The magnificent façade of St Peter's Basilica dazzles in the sunlight.*
◀ *Opposite: Delicate mosaic work, part of the Pontifical Academy of Sciences, in the Vatican Gardens.*

Among the other sculptural masterpieces are the grandiose **Monument to Pope Alexander VII** by Bernini, and the gaunt figure of St Peter, attributed to the 13th-century architect and sculptor **Arnolfo di Cambio**, its big toe polished by generations of pilgrims kissing it. Before leaving the building, take the time to look at the considerable treasures forming the **Museo Storico Artistico** next to the **Sacristy**.

To the right of the main basilica is the lift up to the main roof and portico. If you wish to climb the dome, it is a couple of hundred steps more from here. Many visitors stay in the pleasant Borgo area directly to the north of the Vatican, traditionally where pilgrims stayed in the middle ages.

The Pope gives a blessing to the crowd in the piazza every Sunday at noon, if he is in Rome. To get a place at the Wednesday Papal Audience, *see page 21*.

LA CITTÀ DEL VATICANO (VATICAN CITY)

Excepting the gardens, nearly half of the Vatican City's 42ha (104 acres) is not accessible to the public. The rest of the area comprises **St Peter's Basilica** and **St Peter's Square**, the **Vatican Necropolis**, the museums in the **Vatican Palace** – a 10-minute walk along the perimeter of the palace walls – and a small area of apartment blocks and shops to the north of the piazza.

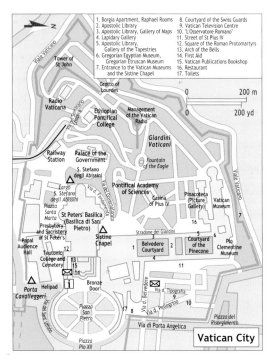

1. Borgia Apartment, Raphael Rooms
2. Apostolic Library
3. Apostolic Library, Gallery of Maps
4. Lapidary Gallery
5. Apostolic Library, Gallery of the Tapestries
6. Gregorian Egyptian Museum, Gregorian Etruscan Museum
7. Entrance to the Vatican Museums and the Sistine Chapel
8. Courtyard of the Swiss Guards
9. Vatican Television Centre
10. "L'Osservatore Romano"
11. Street of St Pius IV
12. Square of the Roman Protomartyrs
13. Arch of the Bells
14. First Aid
15. Vatican Publications Bookshop
16. Restaurant
17. Toilets

Vatican City

Vatican Gardens ★

Well worth seeing to gain a different perspective on the Vatican, the gardens can be visited Monday to Saturdays (except Wednesdays) on a guided tour. The well-established trees, the well-manicured lawns, grottoes, fountains, formal gardens and occasional sculpture create a peaceful ambience. Don't miss the mosaics on the **Pontifical Academy of Sciences** – a gem of a building – and the fine views of St Peter's. Upon exiting, near the **Audience Hall**, spare a moment for the **German Cemetery**, an intimate and pleasant anomaly dating back to AD800.

▶ *Opposite: In the midst of the city, the Vatican gardens provide a lush oasis.*

PAPAL FLIGHTS

The **Pope** has an unusual agreement with the Italian military concerning his travel arrangements. As Italian military personnel do not have the right to step onto the ground of another country, they bring their helicopter into the **Vatican**, land on the Pope's helipad and await his boarding without alighting, themselves, on Vatican soil.

I MUSEI VATICANI (VATICAN MUSEUMS)

The Vatican owns an inestimable wealth of visual arts, which most visitors rarely see for their goal is usually the **Sistine Chapel**, a 25-minute walk from the Museums' entrance in Viale Vaticano. The crowded route to the Sistine Chapel – through seemingly miles of corridors and galleries, (take time to explore the Map Gallery) – hardly encourages the visitor to explore the other great treasures. The nucleus of the Vatican collections came originally from works amassed by Julius II, Leo X and Clement VII, but today range from Assyrian and Etruscan to 20th-century art. Closed on Sundays and public holidays.

The **Vatican Palace** itself deserves note and it is worth lingering at some of the windows or in the courtyard to admire its flowing design. Bramante designed the **Belvedere Courtyard**.

Ancient Art ★★

The Vatican's collection of Etruscan art (dating from the 8th–3rd century BC) is remarkable in its quality and state of preservation. Admire the ancient bronze vessels, the fine bronze statue of **Mars of Todi**, the intricate gold jewellery from burial tombs, the remains of a decorated funeral wagon and the largely intact black and red vases – all remarkable achievements if we consider they were made over 2500 years ago.

Invading Romans pillaged Egyptian works of art as the Empire expanded – hence the many obelisks that grace Rome today – and some of these items are on display near the entrance in the Vatican. Take a moment to look at the mummies, mummy cases and various funerary objects.

The Ancient Romans were collectors – and imitators – of Greek art. The Vatican has a vast amount of statues, including the famous *Lacoön*, the *Apoxyomenos* (an athlete scraping off excess oil from his body) and the *Apollo del Belvedere*. There are hundreds of busts, many portraits of emperors, their family members and other notables. There are also sarcophagi, low reliefs and mosaics that are quite breathtaking in their intricacy.

Pinacoteca ★★

This collection of paintings spans five centuries of art up to 19th-century works and is often a little less crowded than other parts of the Vatican Museums. The Renaissance popes were great sponsors of the arts, and not merely for altruistic reasons. It was, after all, thanks to the popes that such masters as Raphael and Michelangelo were artistically challenged and rose to fame.

THE VATICAN MUSEUMS

To see the museums, go early or pre-book timed tickets (http://biglietteriamusei.vatican.va), otherwise you may queue for hours. Allow at least half a day, preferably a full day, to do the Vatican justice. Admission to the Vatican Museums includes the following:
• **Capella Sistina** (the Sistine Chapel)
• **Le Stanze di Raffaello** (the Raphael Rooms)
• **Pinacoteca** (the Vatican Art Gallery)
• **Museo Etrusco** (the Etruscan collection)
• **Museo Egitto** (the Egyptian Museum)
• **Museo Sacro** (the Museum of early Christian artefacts)
• **Museo Chiaramonti** (the Museum of Greek and Roman sculpture)
• **Museo Pio Clementino** (the Pio-Clementine Museum of Greek and Roman art)
• **Museo Pio Christiano** (the Museum of early Christian sculpture)
• **Museo Gregoriano Profano** (Gregorian Museum of Pagan Art and early sculpture)
• **Ethnological Missionary Museum** (exhibits from all parts of Christendom)
• **Gallery of Modern Religious Art**
• **Biblioteca Apostolica Vaticana** (the Vatican Library, only partially open)
• **Gallery of the Maps**
• **Gallery of the Tapestries**

▶ Right: Fresco fragment of an angel by Merlozzo da Forli, Pinacoteca, Vatican.

Among the most impressive exhibits are the delicate remains of frescoes by **Merlozzo da Forlì**, including the musical angels used so often on greeting cards; **Pinturicchio's** *Coronation of the Virgin*, and powerful works by **Leonardo da Vinci**, **Guido Reni**, **Caravaggio** and **Pietro da Cortona**. Without a doubt, the most impressive work is by **Raphael**; eight tapestries, the magnificent *Coronation of the Virgin* and the *Madonna da Foligno*, plus other paintings would alone assure his ranking among the greatest European artists.

Le Stanze di Raffaello (The Raphael Rooms) **
In 1508, Julius II invited Raphael to decorate four rooms and a *loggia* that formed part of his private apartments in the **Palazzo Vaticano**. The large commission was to take Raphael and his pupils some 16 years to finish and the great master died before the completion of the work. However, the result is an exceptionally fine piece of work imbued with the artistic ideals of the Renaissance.

Last to be painted, the **Hall of Constantine** was entirely executed after Raphael's death to the master's original sketches. The **Room of Heliodorus** is almost entirely by Raphael's hand and depicts semi-religious scenes. The **Room of the Segnatura** boasts, above all, the famous painting, the *School of Athens*, a magnificent work, demonstrating Raphael's mastery of perspective, his understanding of light and a subtle use of colour. Raphael flattered some of his contemporaries with portraits among the philosophical personages in the *School of Athens*. The **Room of the Fire** is painted with the cartoons planned, but not executed, by Raphael.

▲ *Above: A fine Classical carving on rock crystal.*

Galleria d'Arte Religiosa Moderna (Gallery of Modern Religious Art) *

Not as daunting as its sounds, this gallery set out in what was once part of the **Borgia** apartments, displays works of art given to the popes and includes 19th- and 20th-century paintings, sketches and glass by artists as varied as **Giacomo Balla**, **Giorgio Morandi**, **Paul Klee**, **Fernand Léger**, **Odilon Redon**, **Georges Braque**, **Rodin**, **Matisse**, **Graham Sutherland** and **Henry Moore**.

CAPELLA SISTINA (THE SISTINE CHAPEL)

One of man's greatest artistic achievements, the Sistine Chapel was rebuilt as the official private chapel of the popes by Pope Sixtus IV in the 1470s. It was his nephew, Pope Julius II, who subsequently commissioned the talented Michelangelo to paint the famous ceiling, and Pope Paul III who commissioned his powerful *Last Judgment* on the wall behind the great altar. But the marvels do not rest there. The lower walls, too, are beautifully painted by other great Renaissance artists. The Sistine Chapel is also where the **Sacred College of Cardinals** meet when electing a new pope.

RAPHAEL SANZIO (1483–1520)

A giant of the **Italian High Renaissance**, Raphael (Raffaello) Sanzio was born in 1483 to a painter father. He was simply a prodigy and, as a youth of 17, was treated the equal of **Michelangelo** and **Leonardo**, who were mature men. His early formation was with **Perugino**, in Perugia. Here he learned the technique of fresco and, in 1500, received his first commission (now lost). His first signed work was the *Marriage of the Virgin*, in 1504.

The years 1500–20 mark the period known as the **High Renaissance**, when the rediscovery of Classical art and its philosophy reached its peak, largely thanks to these three great masters. Raphael worked from 1504–08 in **Florence** and moved to Rome where he worked until his death. The so-called **Raphael Rooms** represent the apogee of his creative talent.

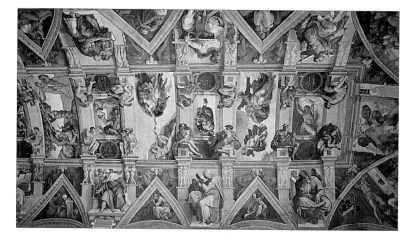

▲ *Above: A magnificent artistic achievement, the Sistine Chapel is well worth the long queues to enter the Vatican.*

The Ceiling ★★★

Since its historic cleaning by the Japanese and its opening again to the public in the 1990s, the now colourful, barrel-vaulted ceiling of the Sistine Chapel has drawn much debate.

Michelangelo shunned all cooperation when he accepted the huge commission and, between 1508 and 1512, worked entirely on his own, often splayed on his back high up on a specially built scaffolding that, it appears, was suspended from the walls rather than resting on the floor.

The 33 frescoes, painted on the curving ceiling between pilasters and supports, depict scenes from the Old Testament, interspersed with large Sibyls (ancient prophetesses) and nude athletes all set in a painted architectural backdrop. These massive forms, often muscular and masculine, sometimes swathed in flowing attire and sometimes entirely derobed, are almost all hymns to the human body (indeed, the nudity in Michelangelo's *Last Judgment* was later painted over by order of Pius IV). Among the best known scenes are the *Creation of Adam*, where the hand of God reaches out to Man; the *Temptation and Expulsion from Paradise*; and the *Delphic Sibyl*, whose face is unusually tender and beautiful.

PICKING A POPE

The position as Bishop of Rome and head of the Roman Catholic Church is lifelong for the pope. Upon his death, all members of the **Sacred College of Cardinals** below the age of 80 are confined in the **Sistine Chapel** until the new pope is decided upon. They meet twice daily to vote and, by tradition, release a stream of smoke from the chimney vent above the Sistine Chapel to communicate the status of their conclave. Black smoke indicates that the cardinals have not yet decided, while white smoke announces the election of a new pope.

The Last Judgment ★★★

This wall fresco rises with frightening intensity behind the great altar and boldly outlines the horrors that await sinners after death. Commissioned by the Farnese pope, **Paul III**, it represents the last great, large-scale work by Michelangelo who died in 1545, four years after its completion. All the saints are depicted here, along with Christ – a simple, beardless figure – against the clear lapis lazuli blue sky. There are several contemporary portraits, too, among the personages.

The Walls ★★★

Below Michelangelo's œuvre are the 12 large wall panels frescoed between 1481–83 by such artists as Perugino (Raphael's master), Pinturicchio, Ghirlandaio, Rosselli and Signorelli. The individual panels show scenes from the life of Moses (on the right facing the altar) and the life of Christ. It is worth lingering here for these paintings are also masterpieces of Renaissance art.

The way back out of the Vatican Museums is somewhat of an anticlimax, but it does pass through some beautiful galleries eminently worth seeing.

THE BORGIAS

Originally from Spain – **Alonso Borgia** was Archbishop of Valencia – the Borgias have a certain notoriety in history and literature. Alonso Borgia was elected **Pope Calixtus III** in 1455 and the family fortunes improved. His nephew, **Rodrigo**, became **Pope Alexander VI** 37 years later. It was the same year that Columbus discovered the Americas and brought back the promise of considerable wealth for the Spanish. Rodrigo's bastard son, **Cesare**, became a cardinal in 1493, but abdicated in favour of a political career. When Cesare's father died, **Julius II** became pope and the fortunes of the Borgias began to flag. So Cesare married off his sister, **Lucrezia Borgia**, first to Giovanni Sforza, then to Alfonso de Bisceglie and finally to Alfonso d'Este, Duke of Ferrara. By all accounts, Lucrezia was a beautiful and cultured young woman and her dubious reputation was largely thanks to her scheming brother.

◀ Left: For decades this artist has worked in the Vatican's map gallery, producing exquisite miniatures.

PALACES IN THE NEIGHBOURHOOD

Adjacent to the graceful church of **Santo Spirito in Sassia** (rebuilt in 1540 by Antonio da Sangallo, who probably also designed the façade) lies the **Ospedale de Santo Spirito**, a hospital and hostel for orphans and paupers that was originally founded around 1200 by Innocent III but was subsequently remodelled by a variety of architects in the late 15th century. It has recently undergone extensive renovation.

Adjoining the hospital is the **Palazzo Commendatori**, the hospital director's spacious residence, which dates from the mid-16th century. The entire complex is a solid testimony to Renaissance architecture and, although it houses a number of interesting medical archives, it still in part functions as a hospital.

A few minutes away on the broad avenue, Via della Conciliazione, you will find the equally solid **Palazzo Penitenzieri**. Built in 1480 and formerly used by confessors at St Peter's, it now shelters well-heeled tourists as it has been converted into the **Hotel Columbus**. In having kept some of the original frescoes and the rather small rooms, the palazzo manages to combine a sense of ancient history with modern hostelry.

Interestingly, the stately 17th-century **Palazzo Convertendi**, just a few metres up the Via della Conciliazione from the Palazzo Penitenzieri, was removed from its original site (where Rafael's house once stood) in the 1930s and reconstructed at its present location. Note, too, in passing, **Palazzo Torlonia** – a fine Renaissance palace that adopts many of the architectural elements of the Palazzo della Cancelleria (*see* page 64).

CASTEL SANT'ANGELO

The rather forbidding round form of Castel Sant'Angelo dominates many views of the River Tiber. Conceived by **Hadrian** (AD117–138) as his mausoleum, it has been re-modelled over the years and has served as a mausoleum for a number of other emperors and their families, a papal refuge, prison, garrison for Napoleonic troops, and now as a museum. The castle is constructed on four main floors with the beautiful papal apartments on the upper two storeys. It is crowned by a huge bronze statue of the **Archangel Michael**, which has given the castle its name.

Access is first by a sloping ramp (that originally led to the mausoleum) and then by the **Staircase of Alexander VI**, which cuts through the building. Most impressive among the various sights are the collection of arms and armoury, the airy and beautifully frescoed **Sala Paolina** and the **Treasury**, on the site of what was probably Hadrian's tomb. A café in the ramparts affords a chance for refreshment and spectacular views over Rome.

Spanning the Tiber in front of the Castel Sant'Angelo is **Ponte Sant'Angelo**, the pedestrian-only bridge also designed by Hadrian in AD134. The flamboyant statues we see today are by **Gianlorenzo Bernini** and replaced the original Roman ones. Open daily.

▲ *Above: Hadrian's Castel Sant'Angelo, with Ponte Sant'Angelo and the Tiber in the foreground.*
◄ *Opposite: The Hotel Columbus backs onto the church of Santo Spirito in Sassia.*

THE VATICAN CORRIDOR

Linking **Castel Sant'Angelo** and the **Palazzo Vaticano** is an intriguing narrow, covered passageway that is built into the fortifications of the **Borgo** area. With only small slits for firing from, it was a protected corridor through which **Pope Alexander VI** (the unpopular Borgia prelate) escaped when the French invaded in 1494 and it was used again in 1527 by **Pope Clement VII**, as Charles V's troops began to sack Rome.

8
Trastevere and Janiculum

Rather different in nature is the area on the left bank of the Tiber, and south of the Vatican City. Trastevere – the name means 'across the Tiber' – is in some ways the most authentic part of Rome today.

Trastevere has few sites to tempt the tourist for there are no Classical antiquities, although there are a handful of interesting Medieval churches with exquisite frescoes. Yet the real attraction lies not in these but in Trastevere's Roman ambience for, in the shadow of the Janiculum, it comprises a neighbourhood of narrow, cobbled streets that breathes character. Life is played out on the streets, music tumbles out through open windows into its alleys, and washing lines string together the sienna and ochre buildings. It has become very fashionable to live in Trastevere, to dine within its ancient walls, and many are the small family *trattorie* that spill out onto the pretty passageways. With its plethora of bars and clubs, Trastevere has also gained a reputation with the social set as one of Rome's popular nightspots.

Janiculum, one of Rome's hills, looks eastward and affords a sweeping panorama of the city from **Piazzale Garibaldi**. On its flanks elaborate gardens and stately villas benefit from a privileged site, while a handful of Renaissance and Baroque palaces were constructed to overlook the Tiber. And beyond Janiculum, the high-rise blocks of Rome's modern and rather monotonous suburbs sprawl westwards to the large green expanse of the parkland around **Villa Doria Pamphilj** and, further, right down to Ostia and the Mediterranean.

DON'T MISS

*** **Santa Maria in Trastevere** and **Santa Cecilia in Trastevere:** see the exceptional mosaics.
** **San Pietro in Montorio:** with Bramante's beautiful Tempietto in the courtyard.
** **Piazzale Garibaldi:** for a panoramic view of Rome.
** **Villa Farnesina:** with its glorious paintings.
* **Botanic Gardens:** take a peaceful stroll in this haven.
* **Trastevere:** enjoy an evening out!

◀ *Opposite: Beyond the River Tiber, Trastevere is of interest for its Medieval remains and also as a gourmand's haven.*

97

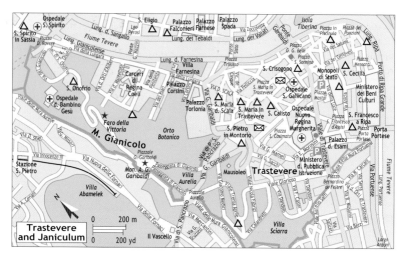

ISOLA TIBERINA

Rome's only island, Tiberina is a slip of an isle in the midst of the River Tiber. It is reached, on the northern side, by Rome's oldest bridge, the **Ponte Fabricio**, which dates back to 62BC, and on its southern side, from Trastevere, by another Roman bridge, the **Ponte Cestio**.

The buildings on this small island are almost entirely related to medicine and healing. After a bout of the plague, an Ancient Roman temple was dedicated to **Aesculapius**, the god of healing, whose sign was the coiled snake, our symbol today for the medical profession. A church, **San Bartolomeo**, was constructed on its ruins in the 10th century. In 1548 the hospital of **Fatebenefratelli** (the 'do-good brothers') was founded and there is still an important hospital on this site today.

Crossing the Ponte Cestio to Trastevere, there is a pleasant walk along the Lungotevere della Anguillara and Lungotevere di Ripa affording fine views of **Santa Sabina**, on the crest of the Avertine Hill on the eastern banks of the Tiber. Alternatively, you could take a stroll through the narrow backstreets from Isola Tiberina Via **San Benedetto**, with its Medieval *campanile* (bell tower), to the **Vicolo dell'Atleta**. Here, in a rather

HOW TO CREATE AN ISLAND

According to legend, Romans decided to revolt against **King Tarquinius** in the early 7th century BC and threw all his grain stocks into the River Tiber. The result was the beginnings of **Isola Tiberina**. If you walk along the embankments, you'll also notice that the island is distinctly boat-shaped.

unassuming Medieval building, now a restaurant, the beautiful, classical statue of the Apoxiomenes was unearthed in 1849, when the building was being remodelled. It now has pride of place in the Vatican.

AROUND TRASTEVERE AND JANICULUM

From Medieval mosaics to modern bric-a-brac, the area around Trastevere has a variety of sights for the tourist to discover, while culinary needs are also well catered for with the many delightful *trattorie* and *caffès*.

Santa Cecilia in Trastevere ★★★

The lovely, peaceful church of Santa Cecilia has an elegant apse mosaic dating from the 9th century, show-ing Christ – flanked by saints – offering His blessing, and underlined by a linear flock of sheep.

Other highlights of this church are an impressive altar canopy by Florentine architect and sculptor **Arnolfo di Cambio**, and the 13th-century fresco remains of the *Last Judgment*, by Pietro Cavallini, in the adjoining convent. Don't miss the very realistic statue of Santa Cecilia in the sanctuary next door.

Wandering southwards, along Via Anicia, you will pass **San Francesco a Ripa**, on the site of the hostel where St Francis of Assisi lodged when he visited Rome. It is also noted for Bernini's moving *Ecstasy of Beata Ludovica Albertona*, another enraptured moment of revelation captured in sculpture.

◀◀ *Opposite: The Ponte Rotto, also known as the Broken Bridge, dates back to the 2nd century bc.*
◀ *Left: Trastevere is probably Rome's most colourful quar-ter. Not only are the narrow streets clogged with cars and motorbikes but buildings are painted warm earthy colours, the streets are decorated with trailing plants and decked out with lines of washing.*

A NIGHT IN TRASTEVERE

Start with an *aperitivo* and some people-watching at **Caffè di Marzio** in Piazza Santa Maria in Trastevere; you may even find a concert in the church opposite. For dinner, head towards **Da Fabrizio**, on via Santa Dorotea 15, tel: 06 580 6244 or **Paris**, piazza San Calisto, tel: 06 581 5378, one of the great proponents of traditional Roman cuisine. For something more innovative, go to **Riparte Cafè**, on via degli Orti di Trastevere 7, tel: 06 586 1816, or if the budget is less ample try the fish menu at **Da Cencia**, via della Lungaretta 67, tel: 06 581 8434 or queue for pizza at **Da Ivo**, via di San Francesco a Ripa 158, tel: 06 581 7082. Try the ever popular neighbourhood trattoria **Il Pastarellaro**, tel: 06 589 6801 – or end the evening with an ice at **Fonte della Salute**, via Cardinale Marmaggi 2–4, tel: 06 8744 0297.

Porta Portese Sunday Market *

Each Sunday morning a sprawling flea market unfolds along Via Portuense and Via Hippolito Nievo around Porta Portese, the 17th-century city gate that was built by Urban VIII. Merchandise such as books, second-hand clothes, bric-a-brac, household gadgets, spices and wholesome foods, furniture, antiques and items of dubious origin are sold to keen browsers and other dealers. It is colourful and full of character.

Santa Maria in Trastevere ***

In the heart of Trastevere, in the piazza of the same name, lies this popular basilica. Its colonnaded entrance, designed by Carlo Fontana in 1702, and 12th-century *campanile* sit tightly between 18th-century palazzi. Carlo Fontana's octagonal fountain in the middle of the piazza has become a gathering point for the itinerant, and unfortunately their ménage does little to enhance the piazza's intrinsic charm.

Santa Maria's origins go back to early Christian times but its form today is largely Medieval. It was reconstructed in 1140 on orders from **Pope Innocent II**, incorporating many granite columns pilfered from Ancient Roman buildings. The mosaic work on the floor is a later remodelling in the Cosmati style.

The basilica is a favourite one for marriages such is its unique and beautiful atmosphere. Above the high altar, the magnificent 13th-century mosaics – including the *Coronation of the Virgin* and a series of mosaics by **Pietro Cavallini** depicting the *Life of the Virgin* – shine in the subdued light.

The narrow roads leading off the central piazza are full of small restaurants, their tables and parasols spilling onto the streets. **Via della Paglia**, alongside the basilica, leads to **Piazza Sant'Egidio**, where the

◀ Left: Beneath the superb Medieval mosaics, the nave of Santa Maria in Trastevere is formed with Classical columns.
◀◀ Opposite: Merchandise of all sorts and authenticity finds its way to the Porta Portese Sunday Market.

Museo di Roma in Trastevere, dedicated to folklore, pageants, festivals and domestic life, is located. Further afield, along Via della Scala, you will come to Via Santa Dorotea. No. 20, a building known as the **Casa della Fornarina** (House of the Baker's Daughter), is where Raphael's beautiful model and mistress is said to have lived.

San Pietro in Montorio ★★

It is a stiff walk up Via Giuseppe Garibaldi to the church of San Pietro, erected on the presumed site of St Peter's crucifixion. The church is decorated by works of some of the Renaissance's great masters and previously included Raphael's *Transfiguration*, now housed in the Vatican. In the courtyard to the right of the church is Bramante's **Tempietto**, a small circular building, crowned with a dome in classical Renaissance style. Recently renovated by the Spanish, it dates from the early 16th century and is one of the architect's finest achievements.

Piazzale Garibaldi ★

On the top of **Janiculum** is the spacious Piazzale Garibaldi, dominated by the equestrian statue of **Garibaldi**. It offers a panoramic viewpoint, with sweeping vistas across Rome, and has become also a favourite meeting point for lovers and joggers. The

GIUSEPPE GARIBALDI (1807–82)

Garibaldi, the great Italian hero, was largely responsible for uniting Italy in the 19th century. He lead a colourful life that started with a criminal record and ended with a seat as a deputy in parliament. Garibaldi fled Italy in 1834 when he was accused of taking part in a plot on the Genoese arsenal. He made his home in Latin America and became involved in the politics of **Brazil**, then **Uruguay** and **Argentina**. Returning to Italy in 1848, he grouped civilians in northern Italy and fought to liberate territory from the **French** and **Austrians**. Following another period of exile, he met up with **Cavour** and moved to unify the country under Vittorio Emanuele II, King of Savoy, championing Rome as the site of the capital. He is best remembered for taking **Sicily** and **Naples** with 1000 followers (the so-called 'Expedition of the Red Shirts') in 1860. In 1870, **Vittorio Emanuele II** became king of the first unified Italy and, in 1874, Garibaldi was elected deputy.

1895 statue recalls Garibaldi's heroic attempts at defending Rome against the French in 1849. The leafy **Passegiata di Gianicolo** leads northwards and then meanders down to **Porto Santo Spirito**.

Further afield, yet enclosed by the city walls, is the **Villa Sciarra**, a pleasant public park which is at its best during the summer months.

ALONG THE TIBER

Two important palaces, Villa Farnesina and Palazzo Corsini, were built along the Tiber by papal families. The gardens of the Palazzo Corsini became the Orto Botanico, a beautifully maintained botanical garden.

Villa Farnesina **

This villa, at via Lungara 230, was originally intended to be linked by a corridor over the Tiber to Palazzo Farnese, and the beginnings of the corridor can still be seen over Via Giulia (see page 62). The villa was originally commissioned in 1508 by the influential banker, **Agostino Chigi**, on land bought from the Farnese family. He commissioned **Baldassarre Peruzzi** to produce a magnificent country retreat, where both mind and body would be nurtured. The villa was acquired in 1580 by **Cardinal Farnese**, hence its name.

Set amid pleasant gardens, the prime attraction at this deep sienna-coloured villa is the stunning ground-floor **Loggia of Cupid and Psyche**, where Raphael painted his sensual frescoes. He was responsible too for the famous

---

CATACOMBS COME TO LIGHT

It was only in the 16th century that the Roman catacombs (see page 109) were found, some 1500 years after they were first dug. In the 1st century Christians were generally buried in common cemeteries, or necropoli. Both St Peter and St Paul were buried in necropoli and later, when they began to be venerated, their bones were disinterred.

▶ Opposite: One of Rome's most pleasant places to relax, the Orto Botanico.
▼ Below: Sunset over the River Tiber, near the tip of Isola Tiberina.

painting *Triumph of Galatea*, in the **Loggia of the Galatea**, where fellow artists **Sebastiano del Piombo** and **Peruzzi** also produced some fine paintings. The **Salone delle Prospettive**, on the first floor, was the work of Peruzzi and has trompe l'œil views of the city. Open daily, but mornings only.

Palazzo Corsini ★

The Palazzo Corsini, a slightly run-down palace (at via della Lungara 10, almost opposite Villa Farnesina) houses the **Galleria Nazionale d'Arte Antica**. The other section of the national art collections is in **Palazzo Barberini** (*see* page 46).

Along with other city palaces, Palazzo Corsini makes up part of the valuable architectural legacy left by the **Riario** family, nephews of Sisto IV. The palace was acquired and remodelled by **Cardinal Corsini** in 1736. Among the works of note in the palace gallery are paintings by **Rubens**, **Van Dyck** and **Caravaggio**. The finely decorated bedroom where **Queen Christina of Sweden** died in 1689 is also of interest. Closed on Mondays.

Orto Botanico (Botanical Gardens) ★

These delightful and well-maintained botanical gardens are not only instructive but also a pleasure in which to pass a relaxing hour or two. A haven from the bustle of a large city, birdlife proliferates and is encouraged by bird feeders and nesting boxes.

Originally, the gardens were part of the **Corsini** property but they were given to the State in the 1880s and today they fall under the auspices of the Department of Biology, University of Rome. **Greenhouses** protect propagated tropical species – such as orchids and succulents – while a series of snaking paths leads you through the **Rose Garden**, **Japanese Garden** (stop to look at the views over the city from here), a garden of medicinal herbs (many of which have been in use since the Renaissance period) and the **Monumental Staircase** with a 400-year-old plane tree towering over the tiered waterfall. Closed on Sundays.

9
Beyond the City Walls

Much of modern Rome extends beyond the ancient city walls, and within the urban area there are still many important sights for the tourist. The large park area of **Villa Borghese**, just behind Villa Medici and Via Veneto, houses three top museums in its **Museo Borghese**, **Villa Giulia** and the **Museo d'Arte Moderna**. The leafy park itself brings a breath of welcome fresh air to the city centre.

Another historic villa surrounded by a park is the **Villa Doria Pamphilj**, country residence of the Doria Pamphilj families. The extensive grounds are a popular recreational spot with families and children.

The magnificent basilica of **San Paolo fuori le Mura** (St Paul's beyond the Walls) is well worth the bus or taxi ride for its lovely cloisters, although much of its interior has been rebuilt.

Further afield, but accessible on a day trip, there are more remains of Ancient Rome. The **catacombs**, of which there are a number on the outskirts of the city, were used to bury early Christians, while **Ostia Antica**, the remains of Rome's port on the Tirrenian Sea, is also a fascinating place to visit.

Seeking respite from the sometimes hot summers, **Hadrian** looked to the hills and, in the middle of the Roman countryside just below the town of Tivoli, constructed his villa and started a trend amongst later rulers, including the popes. The once beautiful **Villa d'Este**, in the heart of modern Tivoli, was built in the 16th century and has wonderful water gardens and grottoes.

DON'T MISS

*** Villa Borghese: quite outstanding museums.
** Hadrian's Villa: the famed home in Tivoli.
** Ostia Antica: a former thriving port during the days of classical Rome.
* The Catacombs: early Christian burial sites.
* Museo d'Arte Moderna: a must for lovers of modern Italian art.
* EUR: Mussolini's great hopes for the Esposizione Universale, and now a suburb of Rome.

◀ *Opposite: Part of the Canopus, at Hadrian's Villa, Tivoli.*

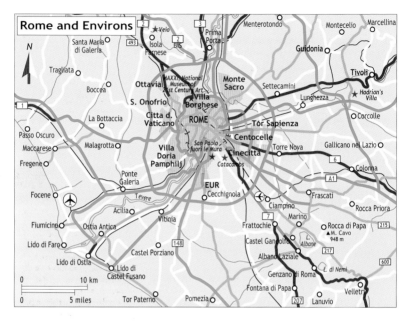

Rome and Environs

Galleria Borghese boasts a fine collection of the master's works. Among the most impressive is the *Giovane con la canestra di frutta*, a beautiful and youthful work. His *Bacchino malato*, the portrait of a young man as Bacchus, by contrast reflects his ill health after being hospitalized. Look out, too, for his works in churches. The fabulous descending angel in *San Matteo e l'Angelo* in the church of **San Luigi dei Francesi**, and the powerful image of St Peter being strung up on a cross in the *Crocifissione di San Pietro*, in the **Santa Maria del Popolo**.

VILLA BORGHESE AND VILLA DORIA PAMPHILJ

Scipione Borghese, nephew of Pope Paul V, commissioned the Villa Borghese in 1605. It was modified over the following two centuries and passed into the hands of the State in 1903. Shaded in parts by centuries-old trees, the park has an artificial lake, statues, imitation Classical temples and a zoo, and is much enjoyed by locals and visitors alike. In season, a tethered balloon offers birds'-eye sightseeing over the city. The Villa Borghese itself is home to a magnificent mueum of fine art, while the Villa Giulia, also in the park, houses the national Etruscan collection.

A modest bus ride beyond Trastevere will take you to the gates of one of Rome's largest recreational areas – the **Villa Doria Pamphilj** and its surrounding parklands.

Museo and Galleria Borghese ***

The ground floor of the villa, the **Borghese Museum**, is a vast repository of sculpture dating from the Greeks to the Romans, and from the 17th to the 19th centuries. Among the most impressive Classical pieces are the *Sleeping Hermaphrodite*, a Roman copy of the famous Greek sculpture; Canova's *Pauline Borghese*, a beautiful nude; Bernini's *Apollo and Daphne*, a sublime marble rendition of the two gods as Daphne morphs into a tree; and Bernini's *David*, reputed to be a self-portrait.

The **Gallery Borghese**, on the first floor, is rich with painted masterpieces, and the rooms are beautifully decorated. Look out for **Raphael's** *Deposition, Lady with a Unicorn* and the *Portrait of Pope Julius II*, his great patron. There are some excellent works by **Caravaggio**, including the *Young Man with a Basket of Fruit* and *St John the Baptist*. Andrea del Sarto's *Madonna and Child with the Infant St John* is a fine example of this talented artist's extraordinary skills. Closed on Mondays.

Museo d'Arte Moderna *

In 1911, numerous pavilions were constructed for the **International Exhibition**, among these **Cesare Bazzani's** palazzo, which now houses the Museum of Modern Art. It hosts the best collection of 19th- and 20th-century works in the city. Head for the **Futurists** and enjoy the works of **Boccioni**, **Balla** and **Severini**, all active prior to World War I. Examples of more modern artists include work by **Giorgio de Chirico**, **Giacometti** and **Giorgio Morandi**. There are also works by other European artists, including **Mondrian**, **Marcel Duchamp**, **Dante Gabriel Rossetti**, **Degas** and **Van Gogh**. Closed on Mondays.

MODERN ITALIAN ARTISTS

At the beginning of the 20th century, Italy was again at the forefront of European Art. A group of Italians living in Paris coined the **Futurist** movement. They wished to glorify men, machinery and movement in art, and the result was a number of radically different paintings, where streaks of colour and repetitive lines create a real impression of dynamism. Some exponents of this short-lived movement (1909–15) are **Severini**, **Boccioni**, **Carrà** and **Balla**. Other acknowledged modern Italian artists to look out for are painters **Giorgio Morandi**, **Giorgio de Chirico**, **Carlo Levi**, painter-sculptor **Medardo Rosso**, and sculptors **Marino Marini** and **Arnaldo Pomodoro**. **Giacometti**, whose slim figures are so distinctive, was, in fact, from Switzerland.

◀ *Left: The Museo d'Arte Moderna has one of the best exhibits of modern art in the country.*

▼ *Below: The Villa Giulia has a priceless collection of Etruscan artefacts, such as this 2500-year-old vase.*

Villa Giulia ★★

Another country residence, the Villa Giulia was constructed by **Vignola**, **Vasari** and **Ammannati** for **Pope Julius III** in 1550. Its particular interest lies in the **nympheum**, a sunken courtyard in Classical style, the reproduction of an **Etruscan Temple**, and the magnificent collection of Etruscan artefacts from a tomb at **Cerveteri** (dating back to the 8th century BC) that form the **Museo Nazionale Etrusco**. Don't miss the sarcophagus of a noble husband and wife (dating from the 6th century BC), the wonderful collection of drinking cups and vases, nor the various decorated, cylindrical cists – the Etruscan equivalent, perhaps, of today's toiletries bag. Closed on Mondays.

Villa Doria Pamphilj and Gardens ★

Created by **Pope Innocenzo X** – a Pamphilj – the Villa Doria Pamphilj is an immense area of greenery, providing lungs to urban Rome. So large and so varied is the topography of this park that one is inclined to forget that it is located in the heart of one of Europe's capital cities. At weekends, it is particularly popular with families and joggers. The villa dates back to the mid-17th century when the pope commissioned **Alessandro Algardi** and **Giovanni Francesco Grimaldi** to build a residence for his nephew, Camillo Pamphilj. It was modified in the 18th century by **Prince Filippo Andrea V Doria Pamphilj** and much of what we see today is the result of this remodelling. Following extensive renovation, the villa's various formal gardens are now open to the public.

THE CATACOMBS AND SAN PAOLO FUORI LE MURA

Rome is surrounded by catacombs. These underground tunnels, hewn out of the soft, volcanic tufa rock, provided meeting places and burial sites for early Christians during the time they were still persecuted. **San Paolo fuori le Mura** is a vast basilica originally built in the 4th century over the burial site of St Paul. Although it is a fair journey outside the city walls, it is well worth the effort.

Le Catacombe (The Catacombs) *

The **Catacombe de San Callisto** (closed on Wednesdays) are among the several catacombs along the Via Appia that are open to visitors. It was here that St Cecilia was entombed, and excavations have revealed the remains of hundreds of thousands of people in its kilometres of corridors. The **Basilica de San Sebastiano** was built over the catacombs where, among others, the remains of saints Paul and Peter were once kept.

San Paolo fuori le Mura *

A fire in 1823 destroyed much of the original basilica and what we see today, impressive though it at first appears, is a heavily restored version, a modern copy or – in the case of the entrance quadrangle – far later additions. There are, however, some exceptions.

▼ *Below: The relatively modern exterior of San Paolo fuori le Mura.*

The marble canopy over the altar is a beautiful work by 13th-century sculptor **Arnolfo di Cambio**, while below the altar are the remains of a 1st-century tomb, possibly St Paul's; some of the frescoes are vestiges of the work of **Pietro Cavallini**; the handsome pascal candlestick is a 12th-century work by **Niccolò di Angelo** and **Pietro Vassalletto**. The only parts to escape fire were the magnificent cloisters, which belonged to the Benedictine convent adjacent. Have a look at the delicate paired twisted columns – absolute masterpieces of Medieval decoration – and the court-yard, which dates from the early 13th century.

MAXXI

MAXXI, the National Museum of 21st Century Art, www.fondazionemaxxi.it This ultramodern museum, designed by ground-breaking architect, Zaha Hadid, is a space for contemporary art, architecture, shows and exhibitions. Located in the Flaminio area of northern Rome, the museum is open Tuesday to Sunday 11:00–19:00, and to 22:00 on Thursdays and Saturdays.

ADRIANO (EMPEROR HADRIAN, AD76–138)

Adriano was born an **Andalucían** in the Roman town of **Italica**, on the outskirts of what is today Seville. In AD117, Hadrian was crowned Emperor in Rome and ruled until his death in AD138. An intellectual with a yen for learning, he set out in AD121 on a marathon tour to observe, first hand, as many of the different cultures as possible that comprised his Empire. In AD122, Hadrian marked the northern boundaries of **Britannia** (England) with a sturdy wall which rose, in parts, to a height of 4.5m (15ft) and extended 114km (70 miles).
Hadrian was a great builder and talented amateur architect. He is reputed to have designed the **Temple of Venus and Rome**, built in AD135, and also his own mausoleum, **Castel Sant'Angelo**. And in Carthage, **Hadrian's Theatre** (another building authored by Hadrian?) is so well built that it still houses opera productions each summer.

OSTIA ANTICA

Ostia Antica enjoyed over 650 years of importance as the port serving the **Roman Empire** and was then cast aside during Constantine's rule in favour of Porto, a newer facility built to the north. After its commercial decline and endemic malaria, Ostia (which once boasted a population of nearly 100,000) was practically abandoned and ultimately became silted up with sand. Thanks to this undisturbed silt, when serious excavations began a century ago, this ancient port was found to have been well preserved.

Ostia Antica's importance today lies with the discovery of its commercial and domestic architecture, consisting of various apartments and small houses. There are also a number of individual villas such as the **Casa di Diana**. As Rome's vernacular architecture has largely disappeared, the discoveries at contemporary Ostia are of immense value to archaeologists.

The **Porta Romana** leads into the town's main street, **Decumanus Maximus**, running through the centre and down to the Porta Marina, the old city gate on the seafront. The ground plans of Terme di Nettuno, or Neptune's Baths, a theatre which has been renovated for performances, offices of the various guilds, and the Forum are all clearly discernible. The grain warehouses, *horrea*, are also well preserved. The temple of Roma and Augustus dates back to the 1st century AD and there are also a number of smaller places of worship (a synagogue and Mithran temples) that confirm the spirit of religious tolerance prevalent in Ostia Antica.

Less classically inclined visitors who want to escape the summer heat and spend a bit of time at the beach, can catch a train for the fast 31km (20 miles) trip to Ostia where, on the **Tyrrhenian Sea**, the **Lido di Ostia** is a popular resort with full beach facilities and plenty of restaurants. The sea is not the cleanest in Italy but it does at least offer an alternative to hot city days.

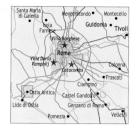

EUR

This area has now become a **satellite town** to Rome. It is easily reachable either by bus or by metro and provides a different view of the city. EUR was begun in 1938 for the **Esposizione Universale di Roma**, which was to have been held in Rome in 1942 (but was cancelled because of World War II). It was taken up again after the war and the area developed into one for both residential and administrative use. Today you'll find an excellent, large shopping centre, **Cinecittà 2** (which has some very good shops), a couple of museums (the Museum of Prehistory and Ethnography Luigi Pigorini and the Museum of Roman Civilization), and the **Palazzo della Civiltà del Lavoro**, which, with its arched recesses, is known locally as the **Square Colosseum**.

◄ Opposite: MAXXI, Rome's new modern art museum, was designed by Zaha Hadid.
▼ Below: St Peter's and Paul's Cathedral in the modern EUR, built for the Esposizione Universale di Roma.

TIVOLI AND HADRIAN'S VILLA

Heading out from Rome along the Via Tiburtina, the highway rises into the **Sabine Hills** which are just 31km (20 miles) from the city, where the small and rather unattractive town of Tivoli is situated. Since the days of the Republic it has been popular with Roman citizens escaping the clawing summer heat and taking the sulphurous waters in its springs.

Villa d'Este *

In the centre of Tivoli lies the Villa d'Este. The Villa was remodelled from an existing convent in 1550 by Cardinale Ippolito II d'Este who also used material from Hadrian's Villa. It is, however, the **gardens** which attract tourists. Powered by the ample supplies of water, the grottoes and fountains, laid out amongst innumerable terraces and the rather neglected garden, are an impressive feat of aqua-technology. Closed on Mondays.

Hadrian's Villa **

It was at the foot of the Sabine Hills that Emperor Hadrian chose in AD118 to site his Villa, a large residential and recreational complex of which little remains intact today. It requires imagination – and stamina – to take in the 120ha (300-acre) site. Many of the sculptures are now in Roman museums.

A scale model at the entrance gives an idea of the Villa's former glory. Of particular interest are the **Smaller Baths**, the large replica of the Athenian Stoa Poikile, now just a grassy arena, the **Canopus**, a beautiful artificial pool surrounded by caryatids and columns which was inspired by the famous sanctuary at Serapis, Egypt, and the so-called **Maritime Theatre**, a circular pool with a central island that was probably a private retreat for Hadrian. Open daily.

CASTEL GANDOLFO

In the **Alban Hills** just 25km (15 miles) south of Rome, and overlooking crater **Lake Albano**, is the small town of **Castel Gandolfo**, better known as the summer residence of the Pontiff. The palazzo in which the Pope stays was built by **Carlo Maderno** in 1624 for **Pope Urban VIII** and was enlarged by subsequent rulers. None of the papal properties are open to the public but the town is very pleasant and the setting, impressive.

INTO THE CASTELLI ROMANI

For a long day's excursion out of Rome, there is a round trip through the area known as the Castelli Romani. This area is essentially **volcanic** and on many of the hill tops you'll see the remains of fortresses and towers, built in the Middle Ages by noble families intent on securing their territory. They used the volcanic craters as a safe 'wall' against possible intruders and today, as well as the ruins, there are also some pretty lakes to discover.

The fertile soil is ideal for this area's active viticultural industry, bottling wine under the Castelli Romani label. The most famous is the white wine, Frascati, named for the Castelli Romani village from which it comes. In Frascati, visit the **Villa Aldobrandini** designed by Giacomo della Porta but built for the Cardinal by Carlo Maderno and completed in 1603. A highlight of this villa is its garden and the views from it. Another well-known local wine comes from Grottaferrata which is also the site of the important monastery, the **Abbazia di Grottaferrata**, built by Greek monks in the 11th century. Its museum is full of interesting ecclesiastical exhibits. Open daily.

Located on the slopes near **Lake Nemi** lies the town of **Genzano di Roma**, renowned for its sumptuous floral festival each June. Here in the town's Via Belardi the **Infiorata** takes place. The street is transformed into a floral canvas, decked out in multi-coloured designs from pavement to pavement with billions of flower heads.

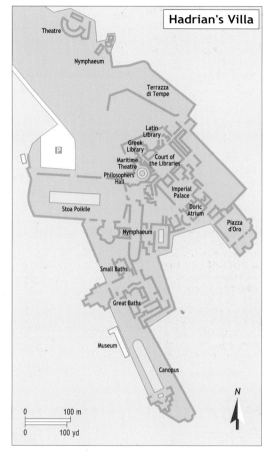

Hadrian's Villa

◀ *Opposite: The placid waters of Lake Albano, just below Castel Gandolfo.*

BEST TIMES TO VISIT

Rome enjoys a Mediterranean climate with cool winters, warm spring and autumn weather, and summer days that can be uncomfortably hot and very crowded. The weather and the gardens are at their best in May and June, and September and October when the flora is in full leaf, and if it rains, it is rarely for long. November to February can be quite cold and rainy but the sights and transport are less crowded. Prices are at their highest from Easter until November, and again at Christmas. July and August are particularly crowded and a time when the Romans, themselves, take a holiday, leaving *chiuso* (closed) notices on their shop and restaurant doors.

GETTING THERE

By Air: Rome is directly linked to all major European cities and many towns in the USA. Direct flights from Rome also serve major cities in Asia and Australia.
The flag carrier, **Alitalia**, via Alessandro Marchetti 111, tel: 02 6666 (within Italy), 00 39 02 6666 (from abroad), www.alitalia.com flies worldwide. Within Europe there are a number of popular low cost airlines that serve the city, such as:
EasyJet (www.easyjet.com), **Ryanair** (www.ryanair.com), **Air Berlin** (www.airberlin. com) and **Air One** (www.fly airone.it). Other major international carriers with worldwide connections include:
British Airways (tel: 199 712 266, www.britishairways.com); **Delta Airlines** (tel: 848 780 376, www.delta.com); **Lufthansa** (tel: 199 400 044, www.lufthansa.com); **Qantas** (tel: 848 359 010, www.qantas.com); **American Airlines** (www. americanairlines.it); **US Airways** (www.usair ways.com). Information for **United Airlines** (tel: 06 6605 3030) can be found on www.united.com
Fiumicino Airport: this is Rome's largest airport, officially known as Leonardo da Vinci di Fiumicino, tel: 06 6 5951 (switchboard), 06 6595 3640 (information), www.adr.it (combined website for Rome airports). Used by all major scheduled services, it is 26km (16 miles) southwest of the city centre.
Trains A direct train runs half hourly, taking 32 minutes, from Fiumicino to Stazione Termini, while a less expensive service runs every 20 minutes between Fiumicino and the suburbs of Trastevere, Ostiense and Tiburtina (travel time around 60 minutes).
Taxis are available from Fiumicino to the centre of town (€40) and, for three travelling together, taxi is the cheapest option. A taxi from Ciampino to the city centre should cost €30–35.

Ciampino Airport: Budget and charter flights tend to use Ciampino Airport (tel: 06 79 4941, www.adr.it). It is 15km (10 miles) southeast of the city centre. There are no direct trains from Ciampino Airport.
Airport Buses: From Fiumicino, Cotral (www. cotralspa.it) operates buses to Magliana and Lepanto metro stations from which visitors can head for central Rome. Inexpensive, direct bus services between the city centre and Fiumicino are run by SIT (www.sitbusshuttle.com), with a stop at Piazza Cavour and Termini (where there is also an inexpensive service to and from Ciampino). From Ciampino, local buses run to the nearby Ciampino Town train station and the Anagnina Metro Station (at the start of Line A – which crosses Line B at Termini offering myriad connections), while EasyJet and Ryanair passengers can book a 40-minute ride on a bus directly into Stazione Termini, Rome, operated by Terravision (www.terra vision.it). Likewise, there is a shuttle service offered by Airport Connection (www. airportconnection.it). Other buses connect the airport with Ciampino Town train station and Anagnina Metro Station, at the start of Metro line A. This takes you via Termini – where lines A and B intersect – onward to the Spanish Steps and Vatican.

Buses also run from Fiumicino to the subway stations of Magliana and Lepanto (60 minutes) every 30 minutes until 21:00.

By Road: Travellers entering Italy by road from northern Europe can do so on toll highways (*autostrade*) from France (via Ventimiglia), various passes and tunnels through the Alps from Switzerland and Austria and, skirting Milan, can continue south on the A1, the **Autostrada del Sole** to Rome. Non-resident cars are forbidden to drive through the historic centre. Visitors are advised to leave their cars in the outskirts or in one of the major car parks, such as Terminal Gianicolo, Via di Porta Cavalleggeri (Vaticano) and Terminal Park, Via Marsala 30/32 (Stazione Termini) as parking in the capital is a nightmare. Visitors arriving by private car require insurance cover (an international Green Card) and must carry the vehicle's documents with them.

By Train: Rome's main station, Stazione Termini has good railway connections with other Italian cities and onward connections to Switzerland, France, Belgium, Germany and the Netherlands. For tourists travelling through Italy (or Europe), one of the various rail passes can be a far more economic way of travelling

the train routes. These include the **Inter-Rail Pass**, which is usually purchased in your home country (in the UK, contact **Rail Europe**, www.raileurope.co.uk). For up-to-date train information look up the national trains website: www.trenitalia.com Termini station has decent restaurants, money exchange, hotel booking service, fast-food outlets and telephone facilities.

GETTING AROUND

Rome has an excellent and inexpensive public transport system. It is also easy to walk around. Bus maps are available from main metro stations and information offices. The best bargain for travel and sightseeing is the **Roma Pass** (www.romapass.it starting at €30); *see* page 120 for more details.

Tickets: A single ticket (€1) on any public transport allows you to change as often as you like within a 75-minute period. The BIG ticket valid for one day costs €4, the three-day BTI ticket costs €11 and the weekly CIS ticket is €16. A single ticket (€1) permits travel in one direction (with changes on all public transport systems to be completed within 75 minutes of validation). All tickets must be bought before boarding and are available from newspaper kiosks, metro stations, some bars and licensed

tabacchi. They require validating on all transport.

Buses: Numerous buses, including eco-friendly methane-run and electric buses are operated by **ATAC** (tel: 167 555 666 or the very good website: www.atac. roma.it), ply the city from 05:30 to midnight daily. Useful buses include the electric buses 116 and 117 near Via del Corso, which cover many ancient sites and modern shopping streets, and bus 64 from Piazza Cinquecento (opposite Stazione Termini) to the Vatican. Bus 590 follows the route taken by Metro Linea A (Vatican to Termini and out to Cinecittà) and offers facilities for handicapped passengers.

Metro: The metro is also operated by Atac (www.atac. roma.it) and comprises three operative lines, A, B and B1, with the forthcoming new Line C due to open shortly. Archaeological remains inevitably slow completion. The metro is open 05:30–23:30, Sunday–Friday, until 00:30 Saturday.

Taxis: These are available from established taxi ranks and can be flagged down in the street. Alternatively, taxis can be contacted by phone but incur a supplement for being called to a hotel or restaurant. To order a cab (in Italian, only), tel: 06 3570, 06 6645, 06 4994 or 06 5551. Taxis are metered, but drivers tend to take you on an extended tour if they think you don't know your way around. **Two wheels:** The adventurous can **hire bikes** and **scooters** to get around town. Bikes are safer and easier to negotiate the narrow streets of Medieval Rome, although the cobblestones don't make for a comfortable ride. Contact **Scooter and Bike Rental** (via Cavour 80a, tel: 06 481 5669, www.onroad.it). *See* also Tours and Excursions, page 121.

WHERE TO STAY

Hotel accommodation in central Rome is among the most costly in Europe, and you pay for the privilege of living in a historic building or ancient neighbourhood. Modestly priced rooms are hard to find, although room rates can be negotiated out of high season (April–October inclusive, Easter and Christmas). Many historic neighbourhoods – such as Campo de' Fiori, Piazza Navona and Piazza di Spagna – do not allow cars without local permits to enter. Parking is non-existent, and the best solution is to arrive by taxi or on foot. If you are visiting Rome by car, *see* page 115 for where to leave your car and use public transport. In the following listings, a double room in the high season is classified as follows: **Budget** €60–125 (at the

lower prices, bathrooms are sometimes shared); **Mid-range** €125–200 (these include private facilities); **Luxury** €200–300. Those well over €250 (and there are quite a large number) are classified as **De Luxe**. A new tax to help preserve ancient Rome is now levied separately on each person per night in the city: €2 for a hotel up to three stars and €3 for four stars and more, to a maximum of a 10-day stay. Visitors arriving by train will find a hotel reservation service at Stazione Termini, otherwise internet hotel search engines (hotels.com or lastminute.com etc.) offer good deals. Lastly, rooms are quite differently priced in low and high seasons.

DE LUXE
Hotel de Russie, via del Babuino 9, tel: 06 328 881, www.hotelderussie.it Stylishly modern boutique hotel; charming garden restaurant and bar and a sybaritic, full-service spa; a few minutes' walk from the Spanish Steps.
Westin Excelsior, via Vittorio Veneto 125, tel: 06 4708 7911, http://excelsior.hotelin roma.com Sumptuously renovated historic hotel with one of the city's finest addresses, gilded décor and a guest list to match.
Hotel Hassler Villa Medici, piazza Trinità dei Monti 6,

tel: 06 69 9340, www. hotelhasslerroma.com Historic, privately owned 5-star hotel with an international reputation and superb location.
Raphael, Largo Febo 2, tel: 06 68 2831, www.raphael hotel.com Impressive, creatively designed 4-star hotel, well-located in a tiny piazza.
Boscolo Hotel Exedra, piazza della Repubblica 47, tel: 06 489 38, www.exedra-roma.boscolohotels.com Ultra-chic, ultra-modern 5-star hotel in the heart of Rome, with spa, garden and roof terrace.
Hotel Palazzo Manfredi, via Labicana 125, tel: 06 7759 1380, www.palazzomanfredi.com Charming small hotel in a renovated hunting lodge overlooking the Colosseum. Wonderful rooftop terrace.

LUXURY
Hotel Massimo d'Azeglio, via Cavour 18, tel: 06 487 0270, www.romehoteldazeglio.it For over 130 years, smart hotels in the classic style. Near Sta Maria Maggiore and Termini.
Hotel Celio, via dei Santi Quattro 35/C, tel: 06 7049 5333, www.hotelcelio.com Small 3-star hotel just behind Colosseum, delightfully decorated in Renaissance themes.
Hotel Forum, via Tor de' Conti 25–30, tel: 06 679

2446, www.hotelforum
rome.com Four-star with
a great location and good
service. Fine views from
rooftop restaurant.
Hotel Condotti, via Mario de'
Fiori 37, tel: 06 679 466,
www.hotelcondotti.com
Attractive small 3-star hotel
with appealing rooms and
good facilities.
Hotel Manfredi, via Margutta
61, tel: 06 320 7676, www.
hmanfredi.com Small ex-
clusive 3-star hotel, decorated
with antiques.
Hotel Columbus, via della
Conciliazione 33, tel: 06
686 5435, www.hotel
columbus.net Former palace
of princes and cardinals, now
a chic 4-star hotel.
Hotel Atlante Star, via
Vitelleschi 34, tel: 06 68638,
www.atlantehotels.com Very
comfortable 4-star hotel with
rooftop restaurant and terrace
for great views of St Peter's.

MID-RANGE

Hotel Locarno, via della
Penna 22, tel: 06 361 0841,
www.hotellocarno.com
Historic hotel with arty period
decor, excellently situated
near Piazza del Popolo.
Hotel Teatro di Pompeo,
Largo del Pallaro 8, tel: 06
6830 0170, www.hotelteatro
dipompeo.it Unusual 3-star
hotel, built on the remains of
an ancient Roman theatre.
Simple, comfortable interiors.
Hotel Nord Nuova Roma, via
Amendola 3, tel: 06 488

5441, www.romehotelnord.it
Well-situated, modernized
with pretty rooftop terrace.
Hotel Campo de' Fiori, via
del Biscione 6, tel: 06 6880
6865, www.hotelcampo
defiori.com Pretty vine-clad
2-star in heart of pedestrian-
only old Rome. The hotel also
has some 12 apartments in
same area.
Hotel Forte, via Margutta 61,
tel: 06 320 7625, www.hotel
forte.com Small, smart 3-star
hotel in excellent location.
Hotel Piazza di Spagna, via
Mario de' Fiori 61, tel: 06
679 3061, www.hotelpiazza
dispagna.it In the heart of
Rome, pretty, charmingly furnished vine-clad 3-star hotel.
Hotel Alimandi, via Tunisi
8, tel: 06 3972 3843, www.
alimanditunisi.com No
better address for the Vatican
Museums. One of two ex-
cellent Alimandi hotels,
complemented by a new,
affordable B&B nearby.
Hotel Sant' Anna, borgo Pio
134, tel: 06 6880 1602,
www.hotelsantanna.com
Just off St Peter's Square,
finely furnished 16th-century
3-star hotel.
Hotel Marghera, via
Marghera 29, tel: 06 445
7184, www.hotelmarghera.it
Excellent value and comfort,
near Termini station.
Hotel Borromeo, via Cavour
117, tel: 06 48 5856,
www.hotelborromeo.com
Smart 3-star hotel in renovated building; good location.

Hotel Bramante, vicolo delle
Palline 24, tel: 06 6880 6426,
www.hotelbramante.com
Beautifully decorated
16th-century inn near the
Vatican. 16 rooms and
some apartments.
Hotel Lancelot, via Capo
D'Africa 47, tel: 06 7045
0615, www.lancelothotel.
com Attractive little hotel
near the Colosseum.

BUDGET

Hotel Mozart, via del Greci
23/B, tel: 06 3600 1915,
www.hotelmozart.com
Delightful 3-star hotel,
small but smart, in excellent
location.
Perugia, via del Colosseo 7,
tel: 06 679 7200, www.
hperugia.it Small but
pleasant 1-star hotel in a
good position.
Hotel Navona, via dei
Sediari 8, tel: 06 6830 1252,
www.hotelnavona.com
Recently renovated 1-star
hotel in an old palazzo, built
on the site of Agrippa's Baths.
Hotel Panda, via della Croce
35, tel: 06 678 0179, www.
hotelpanda.it Excellent location, simple 2-star pension.
Residence Candia, via Candia
135B, tel: 06 3972 1046,
www.residencecandia.it
Small and medium-sized
apartments, just 5 minutes
from Vatican Museums.
Hotel Adriatic, via Giovanni
Vitelleschi 25, tel: 06 6880
8080, www.adriatichotel.com
Situated near the Vatican;

decent 2-star hotel with good-sized rooms.

Hotel Dino, via Milazzo 14, 1st floor, tel: 06 4470 2456, www.hoteldino.net Small, friendly and inexpensive, this hotel is near Termini in a bustling neighbourhood.

Ferraro Hotel, via Cavour 266, 2nd floor, tel: 06 6051 3541, www.hotelferraro.it Small, clean and well-run 1-star hotel.

Hotel Paba, via Cavour 266, 2nd floor, tel: 06 4782 4902, www.hotelpaba.com Intimate, homely and wonderfully central hotel.

Bed and breakfast is a growing industry in Rome, offering excellent, often extremely reasonable accommodation. The **APT** (see page 122) publishes a list of establishments, while www.flatin rome.com offers a range of self-catering apartments.

WHERE TO EAT

Rome is not a cheap place to eat. The only way to eat inexpensively is to buy food in the local supermarkets, or to stick to fast food such as pizza. Expect to pay at least € 30 for a two-course lunch or dinner with wine and mineral water, and more for a more elaborate multi-course meal with wine. Budget restaurants generally cost less than € 25 per person. A meal in a midrange restaurant should be between € 30 and € 60 while

a meal costing more than this is categorized as luxury. All restaurants charge for bread – and many for service too. Most close one day a week, usually Sunday or Monday. Phone to check. In peak season, eat early or make a reservation. The most popular areas for restaurants are Campo de' Fiori, Piazza Navona, Piazza di Spagna, Trastevere and the Ghetto. Restaurants come and go: check out current trends on websites like www.trip advisor.com

EXPENSIVE

Agata e Romeo (nr. Sta Maria Maggiore), via Carlo Alberto 45, tel: 06 446 6115. Famous restaurant, consistently good.

Eleanora d'Arborea (nr. Via Nomentana, northeast of Termini), corso Trieste 23, tel: 06 4425 0943. Worth going the distance, consistently praised Sardinian cuisine.

Glass Hostaria (Trastevere), vicolo del Cinque 58, tel: 06 5833 5903. Cutting-edge, inventive cuisine in innovative interior.

Hostaria Romana (nr. Palazzo Spada), via del Boccaccio 1 (angolo Via Rasella), tel: 06 474 5284. A bit touristy, but smart with good, traditional cuisine.

La Rosetta (nr. the Pantheon), via della Rosetta 3, tel: 06 686 1002. If you fancy fish, this is one of Rome's best places.

Lo Stil Novo (nr. Via Veneto), via Sicilia 66/B, tel: 06 4341 1810. Although new, this modern and elegant restaurant has made its mark.

Osteria Romana (nr. Palazzo Spada), via di San Paolo alla Regola 29, tel: 06 686 1917. Another favourite fish restaurant. Indoor/outdoor dining.

MODERATE

Al Duello (nr. Pantheon), vicolo della Vaccarella 11, tel: 06 687 3348. Modern cuisine served in elegant ambience.

Armando al Pantheon (nr. Pantheon), salita dei Crescenzi 31, tel: 06 6880 3034. Very popular and consistently good.

Gino in Vicolo Rosini (nr. Piazza del Parlamento), vicolo Rosini 4, tel: 06 687 3434. Low key yet very popular because of its excellent cuisine.

Ambasciata d'Abruzzo (Parioli), via Pietro Tacchini 26, tel: 06 807 8256. Copious cuisine featuring Abruzzese's best ingredients.

Antico Arco Ristorante and Wine Bar (Trastevere/Villa Doria Pamphilj), piazzale Aurelio 7, tel: 06 581 5274. Good food and a newer wine bar.

Felice a Testaccio (Testaccio), via Mastro Giorgio 29, tel: 06 574 6800. Very popular, with daily featured dish. Good general menu.

La Taverna dei Fori Imperiali (nr. Colosseum), via della Madonna dei Monti 9, tel: 06 679 8643. Pretty spot with excellent Italian dishes.

Maccheroni (nr. Piazza Navona), piazza delle Coppelle 44, tel: 06 6830 7895. Traditional Roman cuisine at its best.

Pierluigi (nr. Palazzo Ricci/ Piazza Farnese), Piazza de' Ricci 144, tel: 06 686 8717. Busy, bustling and fun. Inside/outside dining.

Piperno Restaurant (nr. Piazza Cenci), Monte de' Cenci 9, tel: 06 6880 6629. Perennial favourite with Romans.

Spirito DiVino (Trastevere), vicolo dell'Atleta 13 or via dei Genovesi 31B, tel: 06 589 6689. An interesting and good restaurant in an historic building.

Trattoria Bucatino (Testaccio area), via Luca Della Robbia 84, tel: 06 574 6886. Pretty little restaurant, with a good Roman menu.

Trattoria Monti (nr. Santa Maria Maggiore) via di San Vito 13/a, tel: 06 446 6573. Up-market, family-run trattoria featuring Roman cuisine.

WINE BARS
(with snacks/cuisine)

Il Goccetto (nr. Chiesa Nueva), via dei Banchi Vecchi 14, tel: 06 686 4268.

Roscioli (nr. via Arenula), via dei Giubbonari 21, tel: 06 687 5287.

Cul De Sac (nr. Piazza Navona), piazza Pasquino 73, tel. 06 6880 1094.

Antica Enoteca di Via della Croce (nr. Piazza Spagna), via della Croce 76b, tel: 06 679 0896.

Ai Tre Scalini (beyond Colosseum), via Panisperna 251, 06 4890 7495.

Palatium (nr. piazza Spagna), via Frattina 94, tel: 06 6920 2132.

INEXPENSIVE

Alle Fratte di Trastevere (good value and located in the Trastevere area), via delle Fratte di Trastevere 49–50, tel: 06 583 5775. Closed Wednesdays.

Antico Caffè Greco (Spagna), via Condotti 86, tel: 06 679 1700. An institution – and not just for its coffee. Great for light eats.

Fraschetteria Marini (nr.Termini), via Raffaele Cadorna 9, tel: 06 474 5534. Cheerful and good.

Flavio al Velavevodetto (Testaccio), via di Monte Testaccio 97, tel: 06 574 4194. Popular for its excellent pastas.

Formula Uno (San Lorenzo), via degli Equi 13, tel: 06 445 3866. Some of the best pizzas in town.

Fraschetteria Brunetti (nr. Piazza del Popolo), via Angelo Brunetti 25b, tel: 06 321 4103. Small and quirky. Excellent value.

Il Pommidoro (nr. Stazione Termini), piazza dei Sanniti

44, tel: 06 445 2652. Good honest Roman fare.

La Gatta Mangiona (Monteverde), via Ozanam 30, tel: 06 534 6702. A great place for pizzas.

La Montecarlo (Cavour area), vicolo Savelli 13, tel: 06 686 1877, and:

La Montecarlo II (north of Stazioni Termini), via Alessandria 106, tel: 06 442 4960. Arguably the best pizzeria in Rome!

Osteria dell'Angelo (nr. Vatican), via G Bettolo 32, tel: 06 372 9470. A pleasant and decent place to eat. Evening set menu.

Otello alla Concordia (nr. Spagna), via della Croce 81, tel: 06 679 1178. Typical Osteria with a bustling authentic atmosphere.

Paninoteca Soppieno (nr. Vatican), borgo Pio 149, tel: 08 2487 4761. They only do sandwiches with fresh ingredients. Excellent reputation for a filling and tasty bite.

Roma Sparita (Trastevere), piazza Santa Cecilia 24, tel: 06 580 0757. Excellent reputation for its authentic food. A good address.

Somo (Trastevere), via G Mameli 5, tel: 06 588 2060. Asia, in particular Japan, meets the Med in this innovative restaurant.

Sora Margherita (nr. Lungotevere dei Cenci), Piazza delle Cinque Scole, tel: 06 687 4216. Cheap and cheerful, a famous institution in Rome – get there early for lunch.

Trattoria da Danilo (nr. Stazioni Termini), via Petrarca 13, tel: 06 7720 0111. Inexpensive and wholesome.

Trattoria da Gino e Pietro (nr. Piazza Navona), via del Governo Vecchio 106, tel: 06 686 1576. Excellent pastas and salads.

Vineria il Chianti (nr. Trevi), via del Lavatore 81–82, tel: 06 678 7550. Popular, serving Tuscan wine and food.

ICE CREAM

For details of some of the best ice cream available in the city, *see* panel, page 69.

NIGHTLIFE

Much of Rome's nightlife is traditional – dining out, drinking in a café, bar or *enoteca* – but there are some excellent pubs, clubs and discos, not always in the centre, that pack in the crowds from autumn to early summer (they close in midsummer as clubbers head for Ostia and the coast) and a wide range of concerts, plays, opera and ballet, as befits an international city. The Thursday edition of *La Repubblica* produces a weekly supplement, *Trovaroma*, which lists (in Italian) what's on in town. In summer, a number of monuments (such as the Colosseum) have occasional performances or exhibitions at night.

Cinema: Movies are usually in Italian, but English or original language films are shown at Warner Village Moderno, piazza della Repubblica 45; Intrastevere, vle Moroni 3 (Trastevere); Eden Film Center, piazza Cola di Rienzo 74; and Metropolitan, via del Corso 7. They are also shown on some nights of the week at the Nuovo Sacher, Largo Aschianghi 1, and the Alcazar, via Cardinale Merry del Val 14.

Bars and Pubs:

Goa, via Libetta 13, tel: 06 574 8277. This one is a perennial favourite with live performers.

Zoo Bar, via Bencivenga 1, tel: 339 272 7995. Popular favourite for its varied music styles now in this new location.

Déjàvu Club, via Ostiense 131. This is a one-stop shop for night-time entertainment.

Metaverso, via Monte Testaccio 38a, tel: 06 574 4712. Another popular venue.

Trinity College, via del Collegio Romano 6, tel: 06 678 6472. Irish pub meets disco. A gathering place for Anglophones.

Alexanderplatz Jazz Club, via Ostia 9, tel: 06 3974 2171. Rome's favourite jazz venue with restaurant.

Charity Café, via Panisperna 68, tel: 06 4782 5881. Ideal for tea by day and wine and jazz by night.

SHOPPING

The place to shop for designer fashion goods such as shoes and clothes is the area around and between Via Condotti and Via Borgognona. The Rinascente department stores (*see* panel, page 28) are good for fashion. For fabrics, head to Bassetti Tissuti, corso Vittorio Emanuele II 73, tel: 06 689 2326, and for perfumes try Officina Profumo Farmaceutica di Santa Maria Novella, corso del Rinascimento 47, tel: 06 687 9608. A short way out of town, the Cinecittà Due Shopping Centre (metro: Subaugusta, Line A) is another excellent hunting ground.

TOURS AND EXCURSIONS

Students and pensioners bring ID for reduced price entry to some museums. The best buy in Rome, if you're into history and the arts, is the **Roma Pass** (www.romapass.it). In a 3-day period, this bundle of offers enables the holder two free museum entrances, reduced costs for all other participating museums and sites (and there are many) and free transport on Rome's bus and metro system and a wealth of other useful tourist information. It is available from the tourist offices and participating museums. Currently it costs €25 per pass. Don't include a Monday in your plans as most museums are closed.

Bus Tours: There are lots of 'hop-on, hop-off' bus tours that go by the main sights in Rome and offer commentaries as they travel. They cost around €15–20, lasting 24 or 48 hours, and usually leave from Piazza Cinquecento (in front of Stazione Temini) before passing by some 10–12 different stops. You can board or leave as you wish. If the weather is great, start early as they get overly crowded and you may not have a seat. The companies to look out for include **110**, **Citysightseeing Roma**, **Ciao Roma**, **Green Line** or **Rome Open Tour**. The **Archeobus** (€12) is a similar hop-on, hop-off bus, that leaves from Platform E of the Stazione Termini and travels via a number or archaeological sites to via Appia Antica and other more far-flung parts of Rome where you'll find more archaeological sites. There are also **Rome by Night** and **Basilica Tours** in season. Information and tickets from the ATAC information booth in front of Termini Station, tel: 06 4695 4695.

Bike or Hike: Bici & Baci (via del Viminale 5, tel: 06 482 8443, www.bicibaci.com) rents out bikes, scooters and motorbikes – including insurance and helmets in the price.

Enjoy Rome, via Marghera 8, tel: 06 445 1843, offers – amongst a host of services –

guided walking tours around various areas of Rome, and also guided bike tours.
Landimension Travel, via Ostilia 10, tel: 06 7759 1009, www.landimensiontravel.it also runs guided city tours by electric bike.

Boat trips: Battelli di Roma, via della Tribuna Tor de' Spechi 15, tel: 06 9774 5498, www.battellidiroma.it offer guided cruises along the Tiber from Ponte San Angelo.
Tourvisa Italia, tel: 06 448 741, www.tourvisaitalia.com operates 100-minute mini-cruises (board beneath Ponte Umberto I on the *Lungotevere Tor di Nona*) to and from Ponte Duca d'Aosta.

Roma Antica, tel: 320 889 0314, www.roma-antica.co.uk runs fascinating walking tours with highly qualified guides.

Bioparco di Roma, Villa Borghese, Ple del Giardino Zoologico 1, tel: 06 360 8211, www.bioparco.it This attractive zoo, at the top of the Villa Borghese park, is fun for kids who may need a break from Rome's history.
Tickets: The **Archeologica Card**, available from particip-

ating sights and museums, is a €22, 7-day pass to many of the top archaeological sights and museums, including the Colosseum. Online ticket purchase for the Sistine Chapel, Vatican Museums and more can be found at http://mv.vatican.va/3_EN/pages/MV_Home.html Alternatively, http://en/roma.waf.it is useful for similar prebooking for museum visits: it all beats waiting in a long queue.

Embassies/consulates:
Australia, via Antonio Boscio 5, tel: 06852 721.
Canada, via Salaria 243, tel: 06 854 441.
Ireland, piazza Campitelli 3, tel: 06 697 9121.
New Zealand, via Clitunno 44, tel: 06 853 7501.
US Embassy, via Veneto 119, tel: 06 46741;
US Consulate, next door at via Veneto 121.
United Kingdom, via XX Settembre 80a, tel: 06 4220 0001, www.british embassy.gov.uk
South Africa, via Tanaro 14, tel: 06 852 541.

ROME	J	F	M	A	M	J	J	A	S	O	N	D
AVERAGE TEMP. °C	11	12	15	18	23	27	30	29	2	22	15	12
AVERAGE TEMP. °F	52	54	59	65	74	81	86	85	79	72	59	54
RAINFALL mm	58	50	44	66	58	25	12	20	52	80	100	58
RAINFALL in	2.5	2	1.8	2.	2.5	1	0.5	0.8	2.1	3.1	3.9	2.5
DAYS OF RAINFALL	8	9	8	6	5	4	1	2	5	8	11	10

Travel Tips

Tourist Information

The **Italian State Tourist Office** (www.enit.it) operates in a number of major cities including: **UK**, 1 Princes Street, London, W1B 2AY, tel: 020 7408 1254; **Australia**, Level 4, 46 Market Street, Sydney, tel: 02 9262 1666; **Canada**, 110 Yonge Street, Suite 503, Toronto M5C 1T4, Ontario, tel: 416 925 4882; **New York**, 630 Fifth Avenue, Suite 1565, NY 100111, tel: 212 245 5618, (offices also in Chicago and Los Angeles). These offices provide information on Italy and Rome, some of it in the form of brochures, and the rest directs you to the internet. Check out www.vatican.va (for museums and cultural information concerning the Vatican); www.turismoroma.it (an excellent site created by the city of Rome); the very useful website, www.rome.info (a privately run site); www.romeguide.it; and the Ministry of Culture at www.beni culturali.it for information on the city's cultural sights. Alternatively, on arrival pick up a free city map and head for one of the following information centres: **APT** (the Rome tourism office) is located at via Parigi 11, tel: 06 448 8991, and is open 09:00–19:00, Monday–Saturday. They also operate an office at the airport, tel: 06 65951, from 09:00–19:00 daily.

The city of Rome runs some nine tourist information kiosks around town, which operate from 09:30–19:30 daily. The most useful ones are at Castel Sant'Angelo, Via del Tritone (second floor of La Rinascente), Stazione Termini, Via del Corso (Largo Goldoni) and Piazza Sonnino in Trastevere. The free monthly publication, *un Ospite a Roma* (which has combined with the former *Evento*), offers up-to-date entertainment listings in both Italian and English and will be found in most of the better hotels in the city – or online at www.unospitearoma.it There is no tourist office offering information on the whole of Italy.

Entry Requirements

To enter the country, visitors from EU countries require a valid national identity card or a passport – valid for a further six months after arrival. All other visitors require a valid passport. Most non EU citizens wishing to stay longer than 90 days will require a visa, as do some other nationals. If in doubt, check with your local embassy.

Customs

Customs regulations for goods bought duty-paid within the EU citizens are fairly generous. 800 cigarettes, 200 cigars or 1kg (2.2 lb) tobacco, 10 litres (16 pints) spirits, 90 litres (120 standard bottles) wine and 100 (160 pints) litres of beer. For goods bought duty-free or outside the EU, the limits are: 400 cigarettes, 100 cigars, 1 litre spirits or 2 litres (just under three standard bottles) wine.

Health Requirements

There are no special health requirements for entry into Italy. If you have a medical emergency, *see* **Health Services**, on page 125.

Getting There

See page 114.

What to Pack

For the winter months (November to March), bring warm clothing, a collapsible umbrella and a mackintosh or light rain jacket. Budget and moderately priced hotels are not always well heated so bring warm bedding and an extra pair of socks. Spring and autumn days can be either cool or warm so layered clothing is best. A showerproof jacket is useful. Summer clothing should be light, with a jacket or cardigan for evening. Most restaurants, except the most exclusive, do not require tie and jacket. Rome's pavements are often made of cobblestone, which are very harsh on the feet. Trainers or flat shoes are most suitable.

Money Matters

Currency: The Italian currency is the euro (€), split into 100 cents. An espresso at a bar costs around €1 and a bottle of mineral water, €2. The smallest coin is 1c; the most useful, the two-colour €1. Paper money starts with €5 and continues with 10, 20, 50, 100, 200 and 500 euro notes.

Exchange rates: The currency is now the same throughout the 17 countries of the Eurozone. Elsewhere, including the United Kingdom and United States, rates fluctuate on a daily basis, although they are relatively stable. Approximately, €1 is the equivalent of US$1.30, and worth about £0.80 depending on the current rate of exchange. To exchange money, you can use one of the many exchange offices where you see the sign *cambio*, as the service is generally far simpler than that of a bank. They are

also much quicker and have longer opening hours, but they do take a rather large percentage for a transaction. Read the small print first. **American Express** (open Monday–Saturday) at piazza di Spagna 38, tel: 06 67641, will exchange cheques and foreign currency. By far the easiest way of obtaining currencies is from a *bancomat*, an automatic telling machine (ATM), using your credit or debit card and PIN number. All major banks offer this service – usually for a small fee. You will find ATMs in Piazza di Spagna, Termini, Via Nazionale, Via Cavour, Vatican and Corso.

Lost (or stolen) credit cards should be reported immediately to the respective issuing organization. AMEX, tel: 06 72282; Diner's Club, tel: 800 864 064 (toll free); Mastercard and Visa, tel: 800 819 014 (toll free).

Accommodation

It is not easy to find quality, inexpensive accommodation. As the so-called high season runs for some eight months, rooms are always in demand. It is therefore important to reserve before arriving if you want a particular hotel. If you telephone, most hotel staff speak some English.

The most popular areas to find a hotel include Piazza di Spagna, Campo de' Fiori, Via Cavour and the Termini area around the station. Most of Rome's sights and a wealth of restaurants are either walking distance or accessible by bus

from these areas. However, for something less expensive, think of the area around the Colosseum, the north side of Stazione Termini and some of the hotels in Borgo, near the Vatican. Travel time is a little more but that is compensated by some less expensive prices.

In recent years, there has been a boom in bed and breakfast and self-catering apartments, offering cheaper alternatives to hotels. *See* also Where to Stay, on page 116.

Eating Out

Eating out is one of the city's pleasures, and there are plenty of venues from fast food and pizzas, to smart *trattorie* and elegant restaurants. Most restaurants close one day a week – often Mondays – so phone and check first. For budget travellers, take-out pizza venues (buy by the slice) and a *tavola calda* are places to head for. Most restaurants post a menu at the entrance, so check out specialities and prices before entering as bills are often much more than anticipated. Bread and cover charge are always added to an à la carte meal. A service charge is sometimes included and government taxes (IVA, similar to VAT) are sometimes itemized as extras on the bill. Look for restaurants and cafés well patronized by Italians. Restaurants listed in this book (*see* Where to Eat, on page 118) – based on a starter, main course, 250ml house wine, water and bread – are categorized as follows: **Budget** less than €25; **Mid-range** €30–60; **Luxury** over €60.

Transport
See Getting There and Getting Around, pages 114–115.

Business Hours
Food shops and markets start business around 07:30, closing for lunch around 12:30–13:00. Shops reopen in the afternoon around 16:00 until 19:00 or later. Fashion stores, which open Monday–Saturday (and some on Sundays), rarely open before 10:30 and some close for lunch. Others remain open until 19:00 or 20:00.
Banks open 08:30–13:30 and 14:45–15:45, Monday–Friday. Generally (although there are many variations), museums and monuments are open 09:00–19:00, Tuesday to Saturday, and 09:00–13:00, Sunday. Some private galleries operate different hours and close weekly on a day other than Monday. Restaurants usually open for lunch from 12:00, closing around 15:30 or later depending on lingerers; they generally open for dinner at 19:00,

closing at 23:00 or 24:00, sometimes later.

Time
Italy's time is GMT plus one in winter, and GMT plus two in summer. Thus, when it is 12 noon in London on a December day, it is 13:00 in Rome. The 24-hour clock is used in Italy.

Communications
Post: Mail can still be sluggish in Italy, with the exception of the new 24-hour delivery service (at a premium price). It is also slow outbound. Stamps for cards and letters can be bought from *tabacchi* (tobacconists), which are open longer hours than the post office. For packages and other mail, go to the Posta Centrale (Main Post Office) at piazza San Silvestro 19 (open 08:30–20:00, Monday–Friday, and until noon on Saturday, www.poste.it).
Telephones: Mobile phones (*telefonini*) have made a huge impact in Italy, but there are still plenty of public phones operated by both coins or,

more usually, a telephone card (*scheda telefonica*), available from newsstands, post offices and *tabacchi*. Some telephone cabins accept international credit cards and others can even send faxes.
Italy offers Home Direct dialling, and various toll free numbers will link you with AT&T, MCI, Telstra, British Telecom and other international systems and debit your calls to your home account. All numbers in Italy start with a '0' unless they are freephone numbers or for mobile telephones. You need to dial the '0' irrespective of where you are calling from in Italy, including calls within the same town. So, for dialling in Rome, you must dial '06' before the subscriber's number. To dial out of the country, dial '00' followed by the country code and then the city or area code (without the '0' before it), and the subscriber's number. For instance, a London number might be 00 44 20 7 624 8000. Dialling to Rome from overseas, keep the '06' code in the number.
Faxes: These may be sent from the post office, and also from a number of cabins around town.
Internet: There are plenty of internet cafés. Some of the most convenient include Internet Cafè, via Cavour 213; Omnitech, via Cavour 280; Internet Train, Corso Vittorio Emanuele and Piazza Sant'Andrea della Valle 3; Easyeverything, via Barberini 2; piazza Sydney Sonnino 27 and via Napoli 26.

CONVERSION CHART		
FROM	**TO**	**MULTIPLY BY**
Millimetres	Inches	0.0394
Metres	Yards	1.0936
Metres	Feet	3.281
Kilometres	Miles	0.6214
Square kilometres	Square miles	0.386
Hectares	Acres	2.471
Litres	Pints	1.760
Kilograms	Pounds	2.205
Tonnes	Tons	0.984
To convert Celsius to Fahrenheit: x 9 ÷ 5 + 32		

Electricity

The current in Italy is 220V AC and Italian plugs are two-pin, round ones. Adapters are available in electrical stores in most countries, or at large airports on departure.

Weights and Measures

Italy uses the metric system. When buying food in delis, cold meats, etc, are often sold by the *etto* (100g/3.4oz).

Health Precautions

There are no particular health warnings for tourists in Rome. Tap water is safe, if not particularly pleasant, but bottled mineral water is available in all hotels and from kiosks throughout the city. Drinking fountains also offer free and cool water that is safe to drink. In summer, bring sun screen and mosquito repellent. Medical facilities are good in Italy but expensive. Take out medical insurance for your trip. If you are from an EU country, you are probably eligible for free emergency medical care under EU regulations. However, you need Form E111 to benefit from this. Obtain and validate one from your local post office before leaving home.

Health Services

For medical help in English, the British and American embassies have good lists of practioners: http://italy.us embassy.gov and http://ukin italy.fco.gov.uk If urgent care is required at home or in a hotel, call Medline on tel: 06 808 0995. For public hospitals

in an emergency, go to International Medical Centre (www. imc84.com), via Firenze 4, tel: 06 488 2371. English is spoken. English-speaking doctors can be found at Rome American Hospital, via Emilio Longoni 69, tel: 06 22551. For pharmaceutical emergencies in English, visit piazza Barberini 49, tel: 06 482 5456 (open 24 hours).

Personal Safety

Petty theft is Rome's main drawback. Bag-snatching and pickpocketing are rife in tourist areas, Stazione Termini and on crowded buses and trains during peak travel times. It is a good idea to carry cash and credit cards in a money belt. Keep belongings in sight (preferably in front of you), wear a camera or bag with a strap across the body, and be aware at all times. It is safe to travel alone in the evening on buses and the Metro but women should not do so at night. We suggest carrying a photocopy of your passport in your wallet at all times and leaving the passport, air tickets and other valuables in safe keeping at your hotel. If driving, do not leave anything inside the car.

Emergencies

If you are robbed, report the incident immediately to the **Carabinieri** (military police) at their *caserma*, or **polizia** (civil police) at the *questura*, or telephone the emergency number **112**. For fire emergencies, tel: **115**, and for breakdown assistance on the road, tel: **116**. For Red Cross Ambulance assist-

TRAVEL TIPS

Road Signs

Senso unico • one-way street
Alto • stop, and *Avanti* • go
(on pedestrian crossing)
Sottopassaggio •
pedestrian underpass
Passo carrabile • don't park
here – the entrance is
constantly in use
Benzina • petrol/gas
Fermata • bus stop
Divieto di sosta • no stopping
Uscita • exit
Questura • police station
Alto • stop
Autostrada • motorway
Pedaggio • toll
Accendere i fari • turn your
lights on
Curva molto pericolosa •
very dangerous bend

ance, tel: **118**. For medical
assistance in English, *see*
Health Services, on page 125.

Etiquette
There are few strict rules, but
wear modest attire when
entering a place of worship.

Language
Apart from the national language, **Italian**, many people
involved in the tourist industry
also speak **English** and **French**
(not to mention **German** and
Spanish). Younger Italians will
usually have learnt some English at school, or from movies
and television. All efforts, however, to speak a little Italian are
always much appreciated.
Grammar and pronunciation
are both logical, but there are
a few things to remember.
'C' is hard (e.g. 'cat') unless followed by an 'I' or 'E', when it
becomes 'Ch' (e.g. 'chair'). 'G'
also remains hard (e.g. 'goat')
unless softened by 'I' or 'E'
(e.g. 'gerbil'). 'CC' is the equivalent to the English 'CH' (e.g.
'church'). 'CH' at the beginning of a word is pronounced
as a hard 'G' (e.g. 'guitar').
If in doubt, use the polite *lei*
(plural) to strangers; you only
use the second person singu-
lar, *tu*, for friends and children.

Disabled Visitors
People are willing to help, but
most facilities are poor and
the area is full of steep hills
and steps, cobbled or uneven
streets and large areas with no
access for cars. It is possible to
get around, but will require
careful planning. For information before you travel:
UK: RADAR (Royal Associ-
ation for Disability and
Rehabilitation), 12 City
Forum, 250 City Road,
London EC1V 8AF, tel:
020 7250 3222,
www.radar.org.uk
USA: SATH (Society for the
Advancement of Travel for
the Handicapped), 347 Fifth
Ave, Ste 610, New York
NY10016; tel: 212 447
7284, www.sath.org
Mobility International USA,
PO Box 10767, Eugene,
Oregon 97440; tel: 541 343
1284, www.miusa.org

Good Reading

Barrett, Anthony, *Agrippina*, Routledge, 1996. Historical.
Brown, Dan, *Angels and Demons*, Corgi Books 2000. Mysticism
and mystery in Rome.
Cornwell, John, *Hitler's Pope*, Viking, 1999. Historical.
David, Elizabeth, *Italian Food*, Penguin, 1998. Cookery book from
the English-language doyenne of European cuisine.
Gibbon, Edward, *The Decline and Fall of the Roman Empire*,
Penguin, 1982. Historical literature.
Graves, Robert and Francis, Richard, *I Claudius*, Carcanet Press,
1998. Accurately documented fiction in Ancient Rome.
Hare, Augustus, *Augustus Hare in Italy*, Michael Russell
Publications, 1977 (19th-century text, re-published).
Harris, Robert, *Imperium*, Arrow Books, 2006; *Lustrum*, Arrow
Books, 2009. The Roman world through the eyes of Cicero.
McCullough, Colleen, *The First Man in Rome*, Arrow, 1992; *The
Grass Crown*, Arrow, 1992; *Caesar's Women*, Arrow, 1997. Finely
researched fiction set in Ancient Rome.
Moravia, Alberto, *Racconti Romani*, Fabbri-Bompiani, 1997; *The
Conformist*, Prion, 1999, Contemporary fiction, translated.
Saylor, Steven, *The House of the Vestals*, Robinson Publishing,
1999. Accurately documented fiction set in Ancient Rome.
Stone, Irving, *Agony and Ecstasy*. Mandarin, 1989, Fictional
novel based on facts about Michelangelo.
Svevo, Italo, *A Life*, Puskin, 1999. Novel, translated.
Yallop, David, *In God's Name*, Corgi, 1997. Finely researched
novel about papal intrigue.

INDEX

INDEX